Ironwill 360° Leadership

Ironwill 360° Leadership: Moving Forward by Douglas Pflug is a captivating journey into the future of leadership in 2025 and beyond, tailored for forward-thinking visionary leaders hungry for success.

Prepare yourself for twelve game-changing trends, from mastering Digital Mindfulness to igniting Purpose-Driven Leadership. Pflug's insights on Remote Leadership Skills, Adaptive Learning, and Inclusive Leadership are your secret weapons for navigating today's dynamic world.

Dive into Resilience, Ensuring Sustainability, and Human-Centric Leadership to discover the roadmap to survive and thrive. Uncover the delicate dance between AI and EQ, unlock the power of collaboration, and master the art of Nurturing Collaborative Leadership for sustained success.

But that's not all—Pflug goes beyond boundaries, introducing Holistic Spirituality and redefining ethical leadership with a universal touch. In a compelling call to action, the book challenges you to be a force for positive change through service, charity, and philanthropy.

Ironwill 360° Leadership isn't just a guide; it's your ticket to transforming leadership into a powerful legacy that resonates with impact and purpose.

Get ready to lead with *Ironwill 360° Leadership*—the future starts now!

Are you prepared to answer the call to action?!

GET READY TO LEAD WITH *IRONWILL 360° LEADERSHIP*—THE FUTURE STARTS NOW!

ARE YOU PREPARED TO ANSWER THE CALL TO ACTION?!

For more information about Doug or details on his book *Finding Your Granite: My Four Cornerstones of Personal Leadership*, please visit www. RiseUpAndExcel.ca.

T0331007

Security, Audit and Leadership Series

Series Editor: Dan Swanson, Dan Swanson and Associates, Ltd., Winnipeg, Manitoba, Canada.

The *Security, Audit and Leadership Series* publishes leading-edge books on critical subjects facing security and audit executives as well as business leaders. Key topics addressed include Leadership, Cybersecurity, Security Leadership, Privacy, Strategic Risk Management, Auditing IT, Audit Management and Leadership

CyRM℠: Mastering the Management of Cybersecurity
David X Martin

Why CISOs Fail (Second Edition)
Barak Engel

Riding the Wave: Applying Project Management Science in the Field of Emergency Management
Andrew Boyarsky

The Shortest Hour: An Applied Approach to Boardroom Governance of Cybersecurity
Lee Parrish

Global Audit Leadership: A Practical Approach to Leading a Global Internal Audit (GIA) Function in a Constantly Changing Internal and External Landscape
Audley L. Bell

Construction Audit: Building a Solid Foundation
Denise Cicchella

Continuous Auditing with AI in the Public Sector
Lourens Erasmus and Sezer Bozkus Kahyaoglu

Ironwill 360° Leadership: Moving Forward: Unlock Twelve Emerging Trends for Forward Thinking Leaders
Douglas P. Pflug

For more information about this series, please visit: https://www.routledge.com/Internal-Audit-and-IT-Audit/book-series/CRCINTAUDITA.

Ironwill 360°
Leadership
Moving Forward: Unlock Twelve Emerging Trends for Forward-Thinking Leaders

Douglas P. Pflug

CRC Press
Taylor & Francis Group
Boca Raton London New York

CRC Press is an imprint of the
Taylor & Francis Group, an **informa** business

Designed cover image: © Lexi Newhook and Douglas P. Pflug

First edition published 2025
by CRC Press
2385 NW Executive Center Drive, Suite 320, Boca Raton FL 33431

and by CRC Press
4 Park Square, Milton Park, Abingdon, Oxon, OX14 4RN

CRC Press is an imprint of Taylor & Francis Group, LLC

© 2025 Douglas P. Pflug

Library of Congress Cataloging-in-Publication Data
Names: Pflug, Douglas P., author.
Title: Ironwill 360° leadership : moving forward: unlock twelve emerging trends for forward thinking leaders / Douglas P. Pflug.
Other titles: Ironwill three hundred sixty degrees leadership
Description: First edition. | Boca Raton, FL : CRC Press, 2024. | Series: Security, audit and leadership series | Includes bibliographical references and index.
Identifiers: LCCN 2024020417 (print) | LCCN 2024020418 (ebook) | ISBN 9781032823485 (hbk) | ISBN 9781032854229 (pbk) | ISBN 9781003518099 (ebk)
Subjects: LCSH: Leadership.
Classification: LCC HD57.7 .P4935 2024 (print) | LCC HD57.7 (ebook) | DDC 158/.4--dc23/eng/20240819
LC record available at https://lccn.loc.gov/2024020417
LC ebook record available at https://lccn.loc.gov/2024020418

ISBN: 978-1-032-82348-5 (hbk)
ISBN: 978-1-032-85422-9 (pbk)
ISBN: 978-1-003-51809-9 (ebk)

DOI: 10.1201/9781003518099

Typeset in Sabon
by SPi Technologies India Pvt Ltd (Straive)

With deepest gratitude and humility, I extend heartfelt thanks to those whose unwavering support has been a constant source of strength during both ordinary and challenging moments in my life. Your love has been a guiding light, shared in both my sorrows and triumphs. My profound appreciation knows no bounds.

To my family, your steadfast support has been the bedrock of my journey. A special acknowledgment to my extraordinary wife, Michelle, and our daughters, Reighan, and Alexis, as well as my future son-in-law, William, and my "fur babies" Riley, Tyla, and Baby Arizona "Zoe."

Thanks to my mother Joan, father Paul, in-laws, Sara and Louis, brother, Don, and his family—Laura and kids Gwen and Abbey. Gratitude also extends to my brother-in-law Robbie, his wife Danielle, and their children, Vanessa and Niko.

Special thanks to my Aunt Joan and Uncle Jim, and, not to be forgotten, my cousins Mario, Trish, Maddy, and Mateo. Each of you holds a crucial place in my life, and I am profoundly grateful for the support and love you've generously shared.

Lastly, to my book creation, review, and editing team, your dedication and personal investment in this project are invaluable. I could not have achieved this without you, and your contributions will live on through the pages of these books.

Trust in knowing that I am committed to making you all very proud: William Brown, Mamta Chail, Bob Guiney, David Hatton, Tuula Jalasjaa, Pat Langdon, Lexie Newhook, Michelle Pflug, and Michael Souliere.

I am who I am because of each of you, and it is my ongoing commitment to reciprocate that love and support. This book is not just about the past; it is a testament to the future and how we navigate the many roles we hold. You have all been a significant part of my past, hold a dear place in my present, and will be ever present in my future.

I love you all!!!!

With heartfelt thanks,

Contents

3 Purpose-Driven Leadership   42

Foreword

With all the changes and developments that have been occurring over the past few years such as remote working, the economic volatility occurring in many countries, and rapid and continuous technology advancements and innovations, Douglas Pflug's book, Ironwill 360° Leadership: Moving Forward: Unlock Twelve Emerging Trends for Forward-Thinking Leaders *is needed now more than ever.*

While leaders of all organizations will receive help from this book, it is an incredible template for small and medium businesses (SMBs) which are the backbone of many economies as they must continuously reinvent and pivot to navigate the challenges, they face often with little to no guidance or support. Therefore, this book should be mandatory reading for every SMB (small and medium) business owner and their leadership team.

Douglas has brilliantly combined his 40+ years of leadership both as a leader and follower across a variety of domains while also leveraging the insights and perspectives of prominent experts and renowned business leaders from a variety of contexts to create this book which will empower, motivate, and guide leaders (new and old) as they move through challenging and unprecedented times in 2025 and beyond.

Moving Forward *begins in Part 1 by detailing key concepts and perspectives that Douglas has identified that serve as the foundation for being an effective leader.*

These foundational key success factors are emphasized and supported by practical tips to aid leaders in reframing their thinking and approach to enable them to succeed in the new environments and challenges they must endure moving forward in 2025 and beyond.

In Part 2, Douglas delves into the critical skills necessary to be an effective leader. His perspective in Chapter 6 on Adaptive Learning I found to be particularly thought-provoking and insightful. In this chapter, he shares his three personal and professional goals to enhance a leader's life.

These are undoubtedly critical to being an effective leader in our continually changing world. As he discusses these goals, Douglas raises some very poignant perspectives leaders should consider adopting but are often neglected or overlooked completely in many other leadership resources.

Throughout **Moving Forward**, *Douglas demonstrates an amazing uncanny ability to combine expert insights—both his own and that of others along with identifying and detailing emerging trends. Douglas then proceeds to provide numerous practical suggestions in his "To-Do" checklists which provide fresh perspectives and approaches to guide leaders' thinking and actions.*

As a result, **Moving Forward** *will not become just another resource "collecting dust" sitting idly on one's bookshelf, Kindle, or laptop. Instead, it will be like one's favorite cookbook—continually referred to, used, and shared to empower leaders to achieve the culture, organizational environments, and outcomes sought after.*

For this on behalf of leaders—new and old, present, and future a heartfelt THANK YOU DOUGLAS! Through this book and your endeavors, you are helping to make the future brighter where all is truly possible!

Michael Haynes
Australia
January 14, 2024

MICHAEL HAYNES

B2B Consultant, Speaker, and Go-To-Market Strategist from Australia

Unlocking Success for Small to Mid-Sized Professional Service Firms

In a decade-long journey, Michael Haynes, Founder of Legacy, The SME Leaders Circle, emerges as a seasoned Business Mentor, Go-to-Market Strategist, and Start-up Advisor. Passionate about shaping triumph stories for professional service firms, he employs innovative strategies in the intricate landscape of B2B customer and marketing dynamics.

Expertise Highlights:

- Strategic Insight: With an extensive background, Michael provides unparalleled strategic insight, navigating professional service firms with precision.

- Speaker and Consultant: Recognized as a sought-after speaker and consultant, Michael specializes in B2B customer acquisition, growth, and retention strategies.
- Go-To-Market Specialist: Excelling in market identification, he crafts bespoke go-to-market strategies tailored to the specific needs of B2B clients.

Distinguishing Factors:

Setting himself apart, Michael delves deep into B2B intricacies. His proprietary framework, "Listen Innovate Grow," fosters clarity, innovation, and sustainable growth, addressing unique challenges faced by B2B companies.

Specializations:

- Market Identification: Pinpointing key markets and clients to streamline business efforts.
- Strategic Go-To-Market Planning: Crafting customized strategies aligned with the unique goals of professional service firms.
- Service and Solution Development: Building offerings that resonate with and fulfill the demands of B2B clients.

Embark on a Transformative Journey:

LinkedIn: https://www.linkedin.com/in/michaelhhaynes/

Preface

"NAVIGATING LEADERSHIP STYLES: A JOURNEY OF DISCOVERY"

Introduction: A prelude to leadership evolution

After the triumph of *Finding Your Granite: My Four Cornerstones of Personal Leadership*[12] and the substantial contribution of $7,000.00 to www.V-eh. ca, the contemplation of embarking on another literary journey persisted for the past six to eight months. The decision to undertake such an endeavor, laden with time, research, and dedication, involved deeply reflecting on the intricate web of leadership styles and their dynamic evolution.

Approximately six months ago, a pivotal question surfaced:

What leadership style do I employ?

In response, I formulated a hybrid approach that seamlessly integrates casual and emergent, as well as personal and professional styles. Drawing inspiration from Bruce Lee's philosophy of "style of no style" in Jeet Kune Do,[3] I advocate for a mindset that explores and embraces diverse leadership approaches, tailoring methods to suit each unique situation and individual.

Bruce Lee's "style of no style" appeared in the 1970s with *Jeet Kune Do*, rejecting the rigidity of competition-focused thinking and emphasizing the importance of personal experience in crafting an individualized approach.

Motivated by recent events, I embarked on an introspective journey, acknowledging the dual nature of such reflection. This endeavor culminated in *Ironwill 360° Leadership "Moving Forward" exploring twelve emerging trends in personal leadership for 2025 and beyond.*

As a leadership student, coach, counsellor, and mentor, I navigated the labyrinth of my own leadership identity. Establishing the tone with this brief leadership overview is crucial, shaping the foundation for the expansive content within this book.

Exploring the kaleidoscope of leadership styles

1. Transactional Leadership or Managerial Leadership: Roots and Rationale[4]
   Transactional Leadership, rooted in exchange, relies on structure, instruction, and monitoring. It originated from Max Weber's ideas and was further developed by Bernard M. Bass in the 1980s. Commonly employed in educational settings, this style sets the stage for hierarchical structures and clearly defined roles.

2. Scientific Leadership: Guiding Through Knowledge and Ideas[5]
   Scientific Leadership involves guidance through knowledge, thinking, and ideas. This style promotes trust, diversity, and clear communication, positioning the leader as a knowledgeable guide fostering a culture of intellectual exchange.

3. Situational Leadership: Navigating Dynamic Landscapes[6]
   Proposed by Paul Hersey and Kenneth H. Blanchard in 1969, Situational Leadership asserts that the proper leadership approach depends on the situation and the individual's developmental level. It supplies a flexible framework for leaders to adapt their style based on the specific needs of each scenario.

4. Principle-Centered Leadership: Prioritizing Ethics and Empowerment[7]
   Stephen R. Covey's Principle-Centered Leadership, outlined in his 1992 book, prioritizes principles, and empowers others. This style emphasizes ethical decision-making, mutual trust, and conflict resolution, creating a foundation for sustainable leadership.

5. Five Leadership Principles: A Blueprint for Exemplary Leadership[8]
   James M. Kouzes and Barry Z. Posner's Five Leadership Principles, detailed in their 1987 book *The Leadership Challenge*, supply a comprehensive framework for exemplary leadership. These principles encompass modeling the way, inspiring a shared vision, challenging the process, enabling others to act, and encouraging the heart.

6. Transformational Leadership: Inspiring and Elevating[9]
   Introduced by Bass in 1985, Transformational Leadership involves intellectual stimulation, individualized consideration, inspirational motivation, and idealized influence to inspire and elevate followers. This style focuses on fostering a culture of innovation and personal development.

7. Servant Leadership: Prioritizing Well-Being and Justice[10]
   Originating from Greenleaf in 1970, Servant Leadership prioritizes the well-being of team members, enriching lives, fostering better

organizations, and contributing to a more just and caring world. This philosophy places the leader in a supportive role, emphasizing service to others.

8. **Transformational Leadership (Bass, 1985): Clarifying the Factors**[11]
Building on the foundation of Transformational Leadership, Bass further clarified the four factors: individual consideration, intellectual stimulation, inspirational motivation (charismatic leadership), and idealized influence. This refinement enhances the understanding and application of Transformational Leadership principles.

9. **Values-Based Leadership (Copeland, 2014): Linking Ethics and Transformation**[12]
Values-Based Leadership (VBL), linking Transformational and Organizational Leadership, serves as the underlying moral and ethical foundation. This style emphasizes the alignment of values with actions, contributing to a principled and purpose-driven organizational culture.

10. **Coach as Leader (Peterson and Hicks, 2018): Bridging Theories**[13]
Particularly relevant for new coach officers, the coach-as-leader approach finds its foundation in all three theories. This style combines coaching principles with transformative and values-based leadership, creating a comprehensive approach to leadership development.

A validation of leadership excellence

I recently completed a 3-course introductory course in Foundations of Management Human Resources[14] at McMaster University in Hamilton, Ontario. The culmination was a Supervision and Leadership course where a compliment from my professor resonated deeply:

> Hello Doug, this is stellar work!!! Fantastic job naming the organizational challenges faced with specific real-life examples. Terrific job naming the leadership approach taken by the leader, supported with specific examples. Terrific examples of what you consider to be critical aspects of leadership. There is excellent value in the skills you shared for effective and successful leadership. Keep up the phenomenal work! You have the traits of a Level 5 leader Doug!
>
> – N.K. MBA

The recognition of having Level 5 leadership traits has ignited my enthusiasm for delving into and imparting these insights within the pages of this book. It is intriguing how our life journey unfolds. I had never envisioned myself as an academic nor aspired to become one. However, with time, I discovered immense comfort and joy in receiving such accolades. One can indeed teach an old dog new tricks.

But what boes it mean to be a Level 5 Leader?

Decoding Level 5 Leadership in 2025 and Beyond.

A Level 5 leader, as defined by Jim Collins,[15] combines personal humility with professional will. They are characterized by a strong commitment to the organization's success, a focus on collective achievements over personal recognition, and the ability to make tough decisions for the long-term benefit of the company.

In the context of progressive thinking and forward-moving leadership in 2025 and beyond, Level 5 leaders offer several benefits:

1. **Long-Term Vision:** Level 5 leaders prioritize long-term organizational success over short-term gains. This vision is crucial for navigating the complexities and uncertainties of the future.

2. **Team Collaboration:** Their emphasis on humility and team success fosters a collaborative and inclusive work environment. This is essential for harnessing diverse perspectives and driving innovation.

3. **Resilience:** Professional will and determination enable Level 5 leaders to navigate challenges and setbacks. This resilience is valuable in an era where adaptability and the ability to overcome obstacles are critical.

4. **Ethical Leadership:** Level 5 leaders often show high ethical standards, promoting trust and integrity within the organization. This ethical foundation is increasingly important in a world where there is increased corporate social responsibility and ethical leadership.

5. **Cultural Impact:** Their leadership style influences organizational culture positively, promoting a sense of purpose, accountability, and a commitment to excellence. This cultural impact is vital for attracting and keeping top talent.

6. **Adaptability:** Level 5 leaders are open to change and continuous improvement. This adaptability is crucial in an ever-evolving business landscape, allowing organizations to stay agile and responsive to emerging trends.

7. **Succession Planning:** By prioritizing the success of the organization over personal accolades, Level 5 leaders often engage in effective succession planning, ensuring the continuity of strong leadership for the future.

In summary, I am incredibly honored to be referred to as a Level 5 leader because they contribute to progressive thinking and forward-moving leadership by fostering a culture of collaboration, resilience, ethics, adaptability, and long-term vision—these qualities position organizations well for success in the dynamic landscape of 2025 and beyond.

> Level 5 leaders channel their ego needs away from themselves and into the larger goal of building a great company. It's not that Level 5 leaders have no ego or self-interest. Indeed, they are incredibly ambitious—but their ambition is first and foremost for the institution, not themselves.
>
> —Jim Collins Good to Great[16]

Harmonizing leadership styles: A symphony of influence

Lastly, I would like to emphasize that I template all these theories with Daniel Goleman's book *Emotional Intelligence*,[17] first published in 1995. This publication significantly contributed to popularizing the concept of emotional intelligence and its importance in personal and professional success.

Incorporating elements from these various leadership styles and using my extensive leadership experience in policing, sports, coaching, mentoring, and counselling, I aim to be a versatile and effective leader, adapting my approach to suit the specific needs and dynamics of different situations and individuals.

This approach is supported by the academic knowledge I have gained thereby earning four separate certificates from Cornell University in Change Leadership, Managing for Execution, High-Performance Leadership, and Executive Leadership.

Conclusion: A call to leadership mastery

> Research your own experience. Absorb what is useful. Reject what is useless. Add what is essentially your own[18]
>
> —Bruce Lee

Figure 1 Jeet Kune Do " the style of no style" —Bruce Lee

Source: https://unsplash.com/@ferventjan

Jeet Kune Do
Using no way as way, having no limitation as limitation

—Bruce Lee

In this hybrid leadership model, I lead, teach, and personally and professionally practice a way, not 'the' way. Embracing the Situational Theory of Leadership (Hersey, 1969), I acknowledge that there is no one-size-fits-all approach. Leaders can adapt their behaviors to meet the unique needs of the situation or follower.

As you explore the pages of this book, my aspiration is that you uncover valuable insights and perspectives to shape your personal and professional leadership styles, reminiscent of Bruce Lee's approach in developing his martial arts philosophy, *Jeet Kune Do*.

Bruce Lee coined the term *Jeet Kune Do* in 1967 to label his martial expression. Despite initial reluctance to crystallize and limit its essence with a name, the practical need for a concrete reference prevailed, giving rise to *Jeet Kune Do*.

Central to *JKD* is the concept of interception, whether intercepting your opponent's technique or their intent. The guiding principles revolve around simplicity, directness, and freedom, embodying the form of no form.

JKD's techniques and philosophies extend beyond combat to address life's challenges. It encompasses physical techniques and applied philosophies, urging individuals to train themselves to their most cultivated state of being. This preparation ensures that when confronted with combat or personal challenges, the required tools are readily available and can be executed without conscious thought.

Jeet Kune Do celebrates the cultivation and honest self-expression of the individual, prioritizing these qualities over adherence to any predetermined and organized style.

Indeed, every great leader possesses a unique set of qualities and engages with diverse types of followers. Recognizing variations in both casual and emergent leadership styles is crucial. Casual leadership refers to day-to-day, informal aspects of leading, where individuals naturally take on leadership roles based on their strengths and expertise.

In contrast, emergent leadership refers to instances where individuals rise to leadership positions based on capabilities and actions, even without a formal leadership role initially. This can happen organically within a group or organization.

Understanding and adapting to these different leadership styles contribute to effective leadership. Great leaders recognize strengths and potential in others, fostering a dynamic environment that encourages various leadership approaches to thrive. Flexibility and an open-minded approach to leadership styles are key attributes for navigating the complexities of leading diverse teams and followers.

Forging leadership evolution in *Ironwill 360°* leadership: Moving forward

> The great courageous act that we must all do, is to have the courage to step out of our history and past so that we can live our dreams.
>
> —Oprah Winfrey

> The best way to predict the future is to create it.
>
> —Peter Drucker
> Consultant, educator, and author.

In the dynamic realm of leadership, where change is the constant companion, the integration of Artificial Intelligence (AI) emerges as a transformative catalyst. This profound force is set to redefine how we navigate our professional and personal landscapes, transcending the boundaries of work and leisure into the future and beyond, notably in the pivotal year 2024.

As a forward-thinking leader and author, I am not just eager but impassioned to illuminate the critical role AI will play and the far-reaching implications it carries for leadership.

> The future belongs to those who embrace the opportunities of artificial intelligence, who see its potential for positive transformation, and who adapt with curiosity and innovation. In the age of AI, the journey of progress begins with open minds and a commitment to shape a better tomorrow.
>
> —OpenAI. (2023). GPT-3.5

AI (Artificial Intelligence) and EI (Emotional Intelligence) "teammates"

Figure 2 AI and EQ working together to improve thought processes for a brighter future

Photo Source: https://unsplash.com/@possessedphotography

In anticipation of 2025 and beyond, I would like to present a comprehensive view of the collaboration between AI (Artificial Intelligence) and EI (Emotional Intelligence) based on emerging trends.

Integration of AI and EI: A futuristic perspective

Emotionally Intelligent AI Assistants: As AI continues to advance, the integration of emotional intelligence into virtual assistants and chatbots is anticipated. This means these AI entities will not only understand and respond to commands but also possess the ability to empathize with human emotions, creating more authentic and engaging interactions.
- Pro: Enhance user experience, foster meaningful interactions, and improve overall satisfaction.
- Con: Raise concerns about user privacy and data security.
- Leadership Strategy: Implement strict privacy measures and user consent protocols.

Emotion Recognition in Human-Machine Interactions: AI algorithms are evolving to recognize and respond to human emotions in real-time. This has significant implications for fields like healthcare, where machines can effectively respond to patients' emotional well-being, particularly in mental health support applications.
- Pro: Revolutionize fields like healthcare, providing effective mental health support.
- Con: Ethical concerns may arise regarding the potential misuse of technology.
- Leadership Strategy: Advocate for ethical standards and collaborate with regulatory bodies.

Adaptive Learning Systems: AI-driven educational platforms are expected to incorporate emotional intelligence, personalizing learning experiences based on individual students' emotional needs. This innovation aims to create a more effective and tailored approach to education.
- Pro: Personalize learning experiences, cater to emotional needs, and enhance learning outcomes.
- Con: The challenge lies in accurately understanding and responding to diverse emotional cues.
- Leadership Strategy: Continuously refine algorithms through collaboration with experts.

Sentiment Analysis in Business: AI tools analyzing sentiment in text and voice data are becoming more nuanced, considering emotional context. This has significant implications for businesses, providing deeper insights into customer feedback and market trends.
- Pro: Provide deeper insights into customer feedback and market trends.

- Con: Risk of misinterpretation of complex emotions.
- Leadership Strategy: Combine sentiment analysis with human oversight.

Healthcare Support: AI applications in healthcare might use emotional intelligence to assess and respond to patient's emotional well-being, particularly in mental health support applications. This marks a shift toward more personalized and empathetic healthcare support.

- Pro: Complement traditional healthcare, especially in mental health applications.
- Con: The challenge lies in maintaining the balance between AI-driven support and human touch.
- Leadership Strategy: Design AI applications to work in tandem with healthcare professionals.

Human-Robot Collaboration: In industries like manufacturing, AI-driven robots might collaborate seamlessly with humans, understanding and responding to human emotions. This collaboration aims to enhance teamwork, productivity, and safety in the workplace.

- Pro: Enhance teamwork, productivity, and safety in industries like manufacturing.
- Con: Concerns about displacement of human workers and ethical considerations.
- Leadership Strategy: Implement training programs and establish ethical guidelines.

Ethical AI Design: Future AI developments are expected to prioritize ethical use, fairness, transparency, and accountability. This shift addresses concerns related to bias and discrimination, emphasizing responsible AI development.

- Pro: Ensure fairness, transparency, and accountability.
- Con: May slow down AI development.
- Leadership Strategy: Foster collaboration and establish frameworks.

Job Displacement: The rapid integration of AI technologies in human resource management has sparked concerns about potential job displacement. As tasks become automated, there is apprehension that certain roles may become obsolete, potentially leading to unemployment for individuals whose responsibilities are automated.

- Pro: Increase efficiency and productivity.
- Con: Concerns about potential job loss.
- Leadership Strategy: Implement retraining and upskilling programs.

Bias and Fairness: The use of AI in HR decision-making processes brings attention to concerns related to bias and fairness. AI systems trained on

historical data might perpetuate biases, potentially leading to biased hiring decisions and concerns about fairness and discrimination.
- Pro: Enhance objectivity and reduce human bias.
- Con: Biases present in historical data may perpetuate biased decisions.
- Leadership Strategy: Implement ethical guidelines and continuous oversight.

Privacy Issues: The integration of AI in HR, involving the collection and analysis of substantial personal data, raises privacy concerns. Employees are apprehensive about how their data is used, who has access to it, and whether it is adequately protected from unauthorized access or misuse.
- Pro: Streamline processes and enhance employee experiences.
- Con: Raise concerns about data usage, access, and protection.
- Leadership Strategy: Establish clear policies on data handling.

Lack of Human Touch: HR, dealing with human emotions and complex interpersonal relationships, raises fears about a potential lack of human touch with increased reliance on AI. The concern is that machines may struggle to interpret and respond appropriately to nuanced human emotions.
- Pro: AI can handle repetitive tasks, allowing HR professionals to focus on human-centric aspects.
- Con: Concerns arise about a potential lack of empathy and understanding.
- Leadership Strategy: Emphasize a balanced approach, integrating AI for efficiency while preserving human interactions.

Transparency and Accountability: The complexity of AI decision-making processes, often seen as "black boxes," raises concerns about transparency and accountability, particularly in critical HR decisions.
- Pro: Enhance consistency and objectivity in decision-making.
- Con: Lack of transparency in AI decision-making processes.
- Leadership Strategy: Establish transparent practices and foster accountability.

Skills Gap: The introduction of AI in the workplace may require employees to acquire new skills, raising concerns about potential skill gaps and job insecurity.
- Pro: AI integration can open opportunities for professional growth.
- Con: Concerns about employees struggling to adapt to new skills.
- Leadership Strategy: Implement proactive training programs.

Overreliance on Technology: The benefits of AI in enhancing decision-making processes raise concerns about overreliance on technology, potentially undervaluing critical human judgment, and intuition.

- Pro: Enhance decision-making processes and efficiency.
- Con: May undervalue critical human judgment and intuition.
- Leadership Strategy: Advocate for a balanced approach.

Ethical Dilemmas: HR decisions often involve ethical considerations, and the integration of AI may introduce complexities in ethical decision-making.
- Pro: AI can contribute to ethical decision-making.
- Con: AI systems may struggle with ethical considerations.
- Leadership Strategy: Prioritize ethical AI design.

Empathy and Understanding: Emotional intelligence enables individuals to connect with others on a deeper level by empathizing and understanding their emotions. This is vital in interpersonal relationships, conflict resolution, and effective communication.
- Pro: EI fosters genuine empathy and positive relationships.
- Con: AI lacks genuine empathy and may struggle to comprehend human emotions.
- Leadership Strategy: Emphasize the importance of emotional intelligence training.

Complex Problem Solving: Emotional intelligence contributes to complex problem-solving by considering not only logical aspects but also the emotional dimensions of a situation. This is particularly crucial in leadership roles and teamwork.
- Pro: EI enhances problem-solving by considering emotional nuances.
- Con: AI may struggle with the complexities of human emotions.
- Leadership Strategy: Integrate emotional intelligence training.

Adaptability and Flexibility: Emotional intelligence is linked to adaptability and flexibility in various situations. Individuals with high emotional intelligence can navigate change, uncertainty, and unexpected challenges more effectively.
- Pro: EI enhances adaptability and resilience.
- Con: AI systems may lack adaptability compared to humans.
- Leadership Strategy: Promote emotional intelligence as a core competency.

Building Relationships: Emotional intelligence is key in building and maintaining positive relationships. It involves skills such as active listening, effective communication, and conflict resolution, contributing to the development of strong interpersonal connections.
- Pro: EI enhances relationship-building skills.
- Con: AI cannot form genuine emotional connections.
- Leadership Strategy: Integrate emotional intelligence training into team-building programs.

Moral and Ethical Decision-Making: Emotional intelligence is associated with ethical decision-making and moral reasoning, involving considerations of the impact of decisions on others and understanding the ethical implications of choices.

- Pro: EI contributes to ethical decision-making.
- Con: AI systems lack an inherent moral compass.
- Leadership Strategy: Emphasize the integration of emotional intelligence in ethics training.

Enhanced Interpersonal Relationships: Emotional intelligence empowers leaders to navigate and manage their own emotions effectively, fostering an understanding and connection with the emotions of others. This skill is vital for developing positive interpersonal relationships, especially in diverse and interconnected environments.

- Pro: EI contributes to creating meaningful connections.
- Con: AI cannot manage emotions or form genuine connections.
- Leadership Strategy: Integrate emotional intelligence training into leadership development programs.

Effective Communication: Emotional intelligence plays a crucial role in effective communication by allowing leaders to express thoughts clearly, and empathetically, and to understand the emotions underlying messages. This is particularly significant in diverse and global teams where communication is foundational.

- Pro: EI contributes to clear and empathetic communication.
- Con: AI may struggle to comprehend emotional nuances.
- Leadership Strategy: Incorporate emotional intelligence modules into communication training.

Conflict Resolution: Emotional intelligence equips leaders with the ability to navigate conflicts with finesse, understanding the emotions driving the conflict. This skill is crucial for maintaining a positive and productive work environment.

- Pro: EI enhances conflict resolution by promoting understanding and empathy.
- Con: AI lacks the emotional understanding needed for effective resolution.
- Leadership Strategy: Implement conflict resolution workshops with a focus on emotional intelligence.

Adaptability and Resilience: Emotionally intelligent leaders are better equipped to adapt to the rapidly evolving business landscape. They can manage stress, anxiety, and setbacks, fostering resilience in themselves and their teams.

- Pro: EI enhances adaptability and resilience.
- Con: AI may lack the adaptability and resilience of humans.

- Leadership Strategy: Integrate emotional intelligence training into change management programs.

Employee Engagement and Motivation: Leaders with emotional intelligence understand the emotional needs of their team members, creating a positive work environment that fosters engagement and motivation.
- Pro: EI contributes to employee engagement.
- Con: AI lacks the emotional understanding required for effective engagement.
- Leadership Strategy: Develop leadership programs emphasizing emotional intelligence.

Decision-Making: Emotional intelligence plays a crucial role in decision-making by enabling leaders to weigh emotional implications alongside rational considerations.
- Pro: EI contributes to well-rounded decision-making.
- Con: AI lacks inherent ethical considerations.
- Leadership Strategy: Integrate emotional intelligence into decision-making training.

Crisis Management: Emotionally intelligent leaders provide stability in times of crisis, managing their own emotions and inspiring confidence in their teams to navigate challenges with resilience and agility.
- Pro: EI enables leaders to navigate crises effectively.
- Con: AI lacks the emotional understanding required for effective crisis management.
- Leadership Strategy: Implement crisis management training with a focus on emotional intelligence.

Innovation and Collaboration: Emotionally intelligent leaders foster a culture of innovation and collaboration by creating an environment where team members feel comfortable sharing ideas, taking risks, and working together toward common goals.
- Pro: EI contributes to a collaborative and innovative culture.
- Con: AI may struggle to foster collaboration and teamwork.
- Leadership Strategy: Integrate emotional intelligence into innovation and collaboration workshops.

Conclusion: Shaping a future of possibilities

In summary, as we shape the future of leadership beyond 2025, it becomes evident that the rise of AI intertwines with our trajectory. Embracing this technological evolution isn't merely an option; it's a strategic imperative. Responsible AI practices and clear policies are essential steps to address concerns and create a workplace environment where AI enhances rather than undermines the overall employee experience.

Leaders who leverage AI for societal, organizational, and individual advancement will define their legacy. The synergy between emotional intelligence (EI) and AI capabilities plays a pivotal role in achieving holistic outcomes, acknowledging the distinct contributions each element brings to the organizational landscape. The journey into an AI-powered future presents challenges, but with visionary leadership and the collaborative integration of EI and AI, we can navigate this uncharted territory and shape a future brimming with unprecedented opportunities.

Note: *The Terminator* movie series information is for entertainment purposes. For insights into *The Terminator* series, explore IMDb sources:

1. *The Terminator* (1984) https://www.imdb.com/title/tt0088247/
2. *Terminator 2: Judgment Day* (1991) https://www.imdb.com/title/tt0103064/

Author's note

The information provided is a general overview based on my knowledge and research. It is intended to offer a comprehensive understanding of the potential impact of AI across various domains. This overview draws on a broad understanding of trends, ethical considerations, and the evolving role of AI in different sectors.

For more specific, up-to-date, or in-depth information on these topics, you may want to refer to reputable sources, academic publications, and reports from organizations specializing in AI research and development. Here are a few recommended sources:"

The future of this book: 2025 and beyond

It is my sincere hope that *Ironwill 360° Leadership: Moving Forward* gains substantial traction in all leadership spaces moving forward. My end goal is to host 3-day conferences, inviting attendees to learn how they too can enhance their leadership alongside friends, colleagues, and clients.

The time for change is now.

Will you take the next steps to join me in creating the bandwagon that society will eventually jump on board?

It is truly an exciting time for progressive thinking and forward-moving leaders at www.RiseUpAndExcel.ca will you join me?

Douglas Pflug
Executive Leadership
Cornell University

About the Author

Douglas P. Pflug

Executive Leadership Coach, Police Sergeant (ret.) Professional Strength & Conditioning Coach, Counsellor, Mentor, Inspirational Speaker, and Author.

Douglas P. Pflug concluded his distinguished 28-year career as a Sergeant with the Guelph Police Service on September 28, 2017. Upon retirement, he transitioned to the Ontario Police College Leadership Unit, serving as the provincial coordinator for the Frontline Sergeant (FLS), Communications Center Supervisor (CCS), and Basic Constable Community Policing.

Doug's commitment to continuous learning is clear through his Executive Leadership, High-Performance Leadership, Change Leadership, and Managing for Execution certificates from Cornell University, Ithaca, NY, USA.

In December 2023, he graduated with a certificate in Foundations of Human Resource Management with a 94% average at McMaster University in Hamilton, Ontario.

In 2020, Doug received national recognition as one of Canada's "123 remarkable Canadians," honored by the Governor General with the prestigious Sovereign Medal for Volunteers. This accolade joined a collection of commendations, including the Queen's Diamond Jubilee Medal in 2012, the Governor General Police Exemplary Medal in 2010, and the City of Guelph Mayor's Award in 2016.

Acknowledged twice with Chief of Police Commendations for lifesaving efforts, Doug's contributions extend beyond policing. He excelled in competitive sports, lettering in Varsity Football and Wrestling while attending the University of Guelph. He won thirty-two medals at Law Enforcement Track and Field meets, including a silver medal in the javelin and a bronze medal in the hammer throw at the 1998 World Law Enforcement Olympics.

In 1994, he founded IRONWILL 360 Strength & Conditioning, affecting thousands of young athletes aspiring to play at various levels.

Joining the coaching staff of the Guelph Storm Hockey Club in 1995, Doug served as a strength and conditioning coach and Police Mentor for 28 years, contributing to the success of elite athletes who later played professional hockey. Retiring from the Guelph Storm at the end of the 2021–2022 seasons, Doug served for 28 years, contributing to four Ontario Hockey League Championships.

2000 to 2010, Doug merged his passions, creating the Constable Jay Pirie Memorial Hockey game, raising over $48,000 for the Guelph Wellington Special Olympics.

2009 to 2012, he served as a strength and conditioning coach for Wrestle Canada at the National Training Center at the University of Guelph.

Doug's commitment to his alma mater continued as he joined the University of Guelph Gryphon Football Team in 1995 as a Community Liaison Coach and police peer mentor.

In 2018, Doug and Michelle Pflug set up the University of Guelph Gryphon Football Pflug Family Community Service Annual Award, honoring graduating players with outstanding community service. He retired from this role in May 2022.

Since 1989, Doug has been a devoted supporter of the Ontario Law Enforcement Torch Run and both the Ontario and Canada Special Olympics. He coached the Guelph Wellington Buns Master Rollers Special Olympics Floor hockey team for 14 years, securing three consecutive Canadian Special Olympics Floor Hockey Championships and three silver Medal performances at the World Special Olympics Winter Games.

In 2022, CRC Press published Doug's biography self-help book, *Finding Your Granite: My Four Cornerstones of Personal Leadership*, with all proceeds, totalling $7,000.00, donated to www.veh.ca to provide service dogs for frontline workers dealing with PTSD/PTSI.

NOTE

1. *The Sovereign's Medal for Volunteers*: Named "One of Canada's 123 Remarkable Canadians." The Sovereign's Medal for Volunteers is a Canadian decoration that recognizes the exceptional volunteer achievements of Canadians from various fields. It is awarded to individuals who have made significant contributions to their communities and have demonstrated exemplary dedication and commitment to volunteer service. The medal is a symbol of appreciation for the recipients' efforts in building a caring and compassionate society.

2. *The Queen's Diamond Jubilee Medal*: This is a commemorative medal created in 2012 to mark the 60th anniversary of Queen Elizabeth II's accession to the throne. It was awarded to individuals who made significant contributions to their communities and the country. A committee of three local Order of Canada recipients reviewed and approved the nomination and forwarded it to the Governor General of Canada. The medal is a symbol of honor and acknowledgment for outstanding contributions to public life.

3. *The Governor General of Canada Police Exemplary Medal* is awarded to members of a Canadian police force who have served in an exemplary manner, showing exceptional dedication, courage, and performance in their duties. It is a prestigious recognition of outstanding service and contributions to law enforcement. The medal serves as a symbol of excellence and recognition for exceptional contributions to maintaining public safety and order.

4. *The City of Guelph Mayor's Award* is a prestigious recognition honoring individuals for exceptional contributions to the community through volunteer service. Established in 1997 by Mayor Joe Young, the awards serve as a symbol of acknowledgment for those who go above and beyond to enhance the well-being of Guelph. Encompassing a broad range of contributions to arts, culture, health, mental health, community building, athletics, and the environment, these awards inspire civic responsibility and active participation in volunteer service. They not only recognize impactful individuals but also encourage others to contribute, fostering a stronger sense of community.

Doug's mantra encapsulates his leadership philosophy:

**Leading with my best self,
Modelling the behavior, I look for from others, and
Always creating an environment where others can succeed.
Taking care of yourself enables you to care for others.**

To contact Doug for a speaking engagement:

Ironwill360Leadership@Gmail.com
TWITTER: @Ironwill360
INSTAGRAM: Ironwill360
Website: www.RiseUpAndExcel.ca

Acknowledgment: Cover Design

Lexi Newhook and Douglas Pflug
Douglas Pflug's journey, depicted in this book, mirrors the timeless symbolism of the phoenix rising from the ashes, deeply rooted in ancient narratives. Just as the mythical bird undergoes cyclical regeneration, Doug finds strength in emerging from despair to triumph. The book's white background symbolizes purity in leadership, akin to the phoenix boldly rising from the ashes of despair. Working diligently alongside Doug, Lexi Newhook helped translate his ideas onto paper. Their collaboration, much like the phoenix rising from nothing, gave birth to the cover concept.

In Greek mythology, Doug's story echoes the phoenix's cycle of destruction and rebirth. Like the bird's emergence from ashes, Doug draws resilience from life's continual cycle of transformation.

Similarly, Doug's resilience parallels the phoenix's association with the Egyptian sun god *Ra*, reflecting profound endurance and the perpetual journey of the human spirit.

Symbolically, Doug's narrative embodies renewal and resurgence, showcasing his capacity to overcome obstacles and evolve. His tale symbolizes personal and collective growth, illustrating an ongoing cycle of change and advancement.

Doug's journey serves as a contemporary interpretation of the enduring phoenix symbol, inspiring hope, rejuvenation, and unyielding resolve. His ability to triumph over adversity resonates with the universal themes of resilience and renewal.

In this spirit, *Ironwill 360° Leadership*, @ironwill360, IRONWILL360 (I), and www.RiseUpAndExcel.Ca were born, reflecting Doug's commitment to embodying the phoenix's transformative power.

Lexi Newhook BA
Talent Acquisition/ Industry 4.0, OPEX, Financial Modeling, Lean Six Sigma, Supply Chain, Maintenance & Reliability, Manufacturing & Operations, MOS, Mining, Organizational Design
linkedin.com/in/lexi-newhook-606b91211
Book Artistic designer and creator

Endorsements

Alphabetically listed.

REVIEW #1—BILL BROWN

"*From my experience in high-level coaching and education, Doug Pflug's* Ironwill 360° Leadership *resonates deeply with my commitment to developing resilient leaders. Pflug's seamless integration of mindfulness and technology aligns perfectly with the challenges we face in today's fast-paced digital era. This comprehensive guide provides invaluable insights, reinforcing the importance of purpose-driven leadership. I highly recommend this book to fellow coaches and educators striving to cultivate authenticity and resilience in their leadership journey.*"

Bill Brown MBA
CIO, Lang Innovation Team
FOGF Membership Coordinator
University of Guelph Football
Elementary School Teacher
linkedin.com/in/bill-brown29

REVIEW #2—MAMTA CHAIL

As a Youth Justice Leader, I found Ironwill 360° Leadership: Moving Forward *by Douglas Pflug to be an indispensable guide for navigating the complexities of leadership in 2025 and beyond. Pflug's insights on Digital Mindfulness and Purpose-Driven Leadership resonate deeply, urging leaders to align actions with a greater purpose and effectively manage constant connectivity.*

His practical strategies for Remote Leadership Skills and Adaptive Learning are invaluable in today's rapidly changing world. Additionally, his emphasis on Inclusive Leadership highlights the importance of diversity and innovation for organizational success.

Pflug's exploration of Human-Centric Leadership in a Digital Age strikes a chord, emphasizing the balance between technology and emotional intelligence. His holistic approach, encapsulated in the discussion on Holistic Spirituality, reframes ethical leadership beyond religious boundaries, advocating for authenticity and a commitment to the greater good.

Ironwill 360° Leadership: Moving Forward *is not just a guide; it's a catalyst for positive transformation. Pflug's vision ensures that forward-thinking leaders are not only prepared for the future but positioned to thrive and make a meaningful impact. As leaders, it's our responsibility to heed Pflug's call to action and contribute to the betterment of the world while fostering compassion within our organizations.*

Mamta Chail MA
linkedin.com/in/mamta-chail-93815a23

REVIEW #3—DAVE HATTON

Ironwill 360° Leadership: Moving Forward *is a game changer. AI will force business and leadership to pivot. This book brings a fantastic perspective on how great leaders can embrace it.*
Pflug has woven the threads of traditional leadership skills, and AI, into clothes the cool kids will be wearing.

The future of leadership will need to use both emotional intelligence and artificial intelligence to effectively lead in the new and ever-changing workplace landscape. This book provides insight on how leaders can adapt to the new technology."

David Hatton
linkedin.com/in/david-hatton-52b70815

REVIEW #4—TUULA JALASJAA

Ironwill 360° Leadership: Moving Forward *by Douglas Pflug, tailored for visionary leaders of 2025 and beyond, takes a unique approach to exploring the evolving landscape of personal leadership. With a masterful blend of profound insights, strategic guidance, and practical approaches, Pflug delivers a compelling actionable roadmap for navigating the complex terrain of leadership.*

Pflug's credentials as a seasoned leader and expert in leadership development lend credibility to his work. With a wealth of experience in leadership roles across various industries including his tenure as a CEO coupled with his extensive leadership academic background, Pflug brings a depth of knowledge and understanding to his insights and recommendations.

Each chapter of the book addresses critical facets of leadership, from Digital Mindfulness to Purpose-Driven Leadership, Remote Leadership Skills to Inclusive Leadership. Pflug's ability to dissect these topics and provide actionable insights demonstrates his mastery of the subject matter.

One of the book's standout features is Pflug's exploration of Holistic Spirituality, where he reframes ethical leadership beyond religious boundaries. Emphasizing universal principles of kindness, service, and integrity, Pflug challenges leaders to embody authenticity and a commitment to the greater good and is consistent with his mantra and actions. Moreover, Pflug's conclusions and "call to action" underscore the transformative potential of service, charity, and philanthropy in leadership. By challenging leaders to contribute to the betterment of society and foster compassion within organizations, Pflug inspires readers to make a meaningful impact.

In essence, Ironwill 360° Leadership: Moving Forward *is more than just a guide; it's a catalyst for positive change. Pflug's visionary insights and actionable strategies ensure that forward-thinking leaders are not only equipped to navigate the future but also empowered to thrive and lead with purpose."*

Tuula Jalasjaa
Int'l MBA Finance
Banking & Wealth Management Senior Executive/Advisor
Founder of The Women's Collection
linkedin.com/in/tuula-jalasjaa-53a5401

REVIEW #5—PAT LANGDON

Ironwill 360° Leadership: Moving Forward *authored by Douglas Pflug serves as an indispensable roadmap for real estate executives operating in today's rapidly evolving global market. Pflug's analysis of Digital Mindfulness and Purpose-Driven Leadership proves especially pertinent, offering insights that empower leaders to make well-informed decisions and motivate their teams effectively. Additionally, the book's emphasis on Remote Leadership Skills and Inclusive Leadership delivers practical approaches for navigating remote work dynamics and cultivating diversity within multinational organizations. In sum,* Ironwill 360° Leadership *emerges as a must-have resource for real estate leaders seeking to excel amid the complexities of the modern digital era, providing actionable strategies for success."*

Pat Langdon
Chief Executive Officer - Langdon Partners Real Estate Limited
linkedin.com/in/pat-langdon-53848710

REVIEW #6—PHIL LUE

I have known Doug for 35+ years and having been in Policing for 30 years and counting, I have the utmost respect and admiration for what he is trying to accomplish with this book. Despite his years of service and countless projects, his enthusiasm and energy in creating a top-notch product always impressed me. I believe the finished product will provide all kinds of "leaders" with more insight and methods to elevate their leadership skills. He is more than qualified to author this book as he has honed his leadership skills for years and performed as a Law Enforcement Officer (LOE), trainer, and mentor at a very high level.

Doug has always displayed leadership qualities, even when we were rookies on the Guelph football team. He stood out as one of the people that others naturally gravitate to and follow. As I've said throughout my policing career, you can make people supervisors, but it is very difficult to make people leaders; many leaders just have that natural ability.

This book is relevant for anyone in a management position who is interested in staying current and serious about how they manage moving forward. Additionally, it's valuable for anyone in the law enforcement world who is in a middle/upper management position. Integrating real-world examples/scenarios might make the book more appealing to these types of managers.

Phil Lue
Superintendent
Royal Canadian Mounted Police
University of Guelph Football Alumnus
linkedin.com/in/phil-lue-aa25a4a6

REVIEW #7—MICHAEL SOULIERE

Ironwill 360° Leadership: Moving Forward *is a transformative guide for progressive thinking and forward-moving leaders, navigating the complexities of leadership in the digital age. Pflug's insights into key trends for 2025 provide practical strategies for success.*

The book emphasizes Digital Mindfulness, Purpose-Driven Leadership, and Authenticity as crucial elements. It offers practical advice on Remote Leadership Skills, Adaptive Learning, and Inclusive Leadership, highlighting the importance of sustainability and human-centric leadership.

The balance between AI and EQ is emphasized, stressing the significance of collaboration for innovation. The final chapter reframes ethical leadership through Holistic Spirituality, promoting universal values, such as kindness, integrity, and mindfulness.

Overall, Ironwill 360° Leadership: Moving Forward *is not just a guide but a catalyst for positive change, empowering leaders to thrive in an ever-evolving world."*

Michael Souliere MA
Police Officer (Retired) and Police Instructor
linkedin.com/in/michael-souliere-ma-CA-07466122

REVIEW #8—GREG HUTCHINS

Practical advice for becoming a leader and manager. No fluff. Just good stuff. The material is presented in doable thought bites with practical examples.

Recommendation: Buy this book. Use this book. Become a great leader.

Greg Hutchins PE CERM
Principal Engineer Quality + Engineering
linkedin.com/in/greghutchins

EXECUTIVE SUMMARY

Ironwill 360° Leadership: Moving Forward by Douglas Pflug is a groundbreaking exploration of the pivotal trends shaping personal leadership for 2025 and beyond. Tailored for visionary leaders who are forward-thinking and moving forward, this book navigates the complex leadership terrain, providing profound insights, strategic guidance, and practical approaches.

- Digital Mindfulness: Pflug emphasizes the need for leaders to cultivate Digital Mindfulness, enhancing decision-making in the digital age and mitigating the challenges of constant connectivity.

- Purpose-Driven Leadership: The focus shifts to Purpose-Driven Leadership, urging leaders to align actions with a greater purpose, fostering personal fulfillment, and driving organizational success through inspiration.

- Authenticity in Leadership: Authenticity is identified as a cornerstone, with Pflug delving into the importance of leaders embracing their true selves, fostering trust, and creating a culture valuing openness.

- Remote Leadership Skills: Addressing the rise of remote work, the book provides practical strategies for Remote Leadership Skills, focusing on building effective virtual teams and maintaining productivity.

- Adaptive Learning: In the face of continuous change, Adaptive Learning emerges as a crucial skill, enabling leaders and teams to thrive in dynamic and uncertain environments.

- Inclusive Leadership: Pflug explores Inclusive Leadership, offering actionable insights on fostering diversity, inclusivity, and harnessing diverse perspectives.

- Resiliency Cultivation: Resilience is an essential quality for leaders facing adversity, with practical tools and strategies for bouncing back from setbacks.

- Ensuring Sustainability: Sustainability takes the spotlight, emphasizing the role of leaders in fostering sustainable practices within their organizations for long-term success.

- Human-Centric Leadership in a Digital Age: Advocating for a human-centric approach, this chapter explores balancing technology with a focus on human well-being, empathy, and connection.

- The Heart of Leadership: AI vs EQ: The delicate balance between AI and EQ is navigated, emphasizing the irreplaceable role of emotional intelligence in effective leadership.

- The Synergy of Collaboration: Collaboration emerges as a key theme, examining its power in driving innovation, problem-solving, and organizational success.

- Nurturing Collaborative Leadership: The final chapter provides actionable strategies for Nurturing Collaborative Leadership and building a culture of collaboration for sustained success.

- Holistic Spirituality: Pflug reframes ethical leadership beyond religious boundaries, emphasizing universal good, kindness, and service. Holistic spirituality calls for leadership characterized by authenticity, integrity, and a commitment to the greater good.

Pflug's conclusion and "call to action" highlights the transformative impact of service, charity, ethics and philanthropy, challenging leaders to contribute to the world's betterment and foster compassion within organizations.

Ironwill 360° Leadership: Moving Forward is more than a guide; it catalyzes positive transformation. Pflug's vision ensures that forward-thinking leaders are not only prepared for the future but positioned to thrive and make a meaningful impact.

"BRIEF ENCOUNTER LEADS TO MUTUAL RESPECT AND FRIENDSHIP"

Bob Guiney of *The Bachelor* reviews *Ironwill 360 Leadership Moving Forward, unlocking 12 emerging trends for forward-thinking leaders.*

"When I first met Douglas Pflug, to say I was impressed with the warmth, kindness, and generosity of this larger-than-life personality would be a gross understatement. My wife, our friends, and I had taken a day trip from Grosse Ile, MI, to Amherstburg, Ontario, to show my in-laws the beautiful restaurants and wineries that we all knew a trip to Canada had to offer. It came as a huge surprise to my in-laws, as they are from California. As we often tease, Californians think that they are the only ones with waterways and wineries, so of course, this was a shock!! (kidding...).

As we exited the boat and made our way onto dry land, my father-in-law was struggling a bit with the walk. Before we knew it, this tan, muscular guy was walking briskly down the dock to help take my FIL's arm with me and escort him up to the end of the dock. He did so with such confidence and warmth that it was absolutely impossible to resist or defer. He was going to help, and that was the end of it! He then took my father-in-law straight over to a golf cart, escorted his own family off of it, and proceeded to tell me exactly where to drive the cart—and just to leave the keys in it, and that he would pick it up when we were done—OR—if we'd prefer, we could just keep it there until we got done with the winery tour so that we could make sure my FIL would make it back to the boat without too much issue.

This man didn't know us, but he immediately trusted us with this very cool, tricked-out golf cart... And I didn't think twice about it! This was simply the kindest gesture that I could have imagined greeting us as we pulled up. And my in-laws were completely blown away! As was I! This kind and big-hearted man just changed the landscape of our trip within 5 minutes of arrival... And you could tell by the way he did it—that this was nothing new! Doug just does this kind of thing. All the time! His family wasn't surprised. They seemed completely at ease with the whole thing... And it was beautiful!

I say all of this because it is important to know that someone who chooses to author a book about different styles of Leadership—NEEDS to truly be a Leader. This person NEEDS to know how to engage people, how to respond to people, and how to relate to people. Typically speaking, that first impression is the strongest! It is the moment that an individual establishes themselves as a Leader or as someone who just lets life happen to them. It happens within those first few minutes of engagement.

And I can tell you firsthand, that Douglas Pflug is a dynamic and enigmatic individual. And upon meeting him, I knew that he was truly a Leader of men. He's a man that within a few seconds made an enormous impression on a bunch of people that he had never previously met, and he made a dramatic & lasting impact! And he made a friend in me. My FIL now talks about visiting Canada again, with the hopes that we will spend time with the "big, kind Canadian Policeman" while my in-laws fall in love with all of Canada in 5 minutes! They exchanged Challenge coins, and my FIL cannot stop talking about it! It was a fantastic experience!

Through years of playing sports, participating in different forms of student government, etc., and through being in a position of partnership and management throughout my career, I have come to know that leadership comes in many forms. After my experiences on The Bachelor, *I was put into positions where I was expected to lead people just because they knew me from a TV show. It was, at times awkward, but something I felt comfortable with as well. I just always tried to lead by example. And tried to lead by doing what I wanted or expected others to do.*

This was what I learned from my father and what I try to do every day with my children. Frankly, I didn't know of much else that was an effective form of leadership that I felt comfortable doing. However, I learned of so many more leadership styles by reading Doug's book and realizing that what I knew previously was the tip of the iceberg.

The detail by which Doug goes into these different leadership styles is educational and captivating. From my reading, I realized that there were different ways that I could incorporate some of these approaches, and I feel confident that they would have a profound impact on how people perceive me - and ultimately respond to me in different situations.

As I mentioned earlier, I have always tried to lead by setting an example. And with Doug's approach to his writing, it rings true to me that he does the same. I truly feel that I am reading the words of someone who does just that every day. He leads by example. He lives his life as an example of what we should hope all of our leaders do. Doug is the man who 'walks the walk'. In a few moments on any given Sunday, he made an impression on me and the more I get to know him, the more I know that first impression was spot-on!! He will always have my admiration and respect for how he has lived his life and dedicated it to the betterment of himself and with those whom he comes into contact.

I am honored to have been able to read the chapters of this manuscript before it goes wide. I can tell you that my sincere hope is that more of our leaders choose to read these pages and embody what Doug has devoted his life to... Leading others through service, sacrifice, and kindness.

I hope that this works for you and that you can use it. Either way, I hope you know how honored I am that you invited me to be a part of this and to learn through your work!

Thank you!

Sincerely,
Bob Guiney CLMS
Account Executive, Sales & Marketing - Lincoln
Financial Group
Host / TV Personality - B Good Productions /
Robert Guiney Inc
linkedin.com/in/bobguiney

CHAPTER "TO-DO" CHECKLIST

1. **Continuous Assessment:**
   Regularly assess industry trends, technological advancements, and evolving skill requirements to adapt strategies accordingly.

2. **Robust Reskilling Programs:**
   Implement comprehensive reskilling programs alongside technological integration to equip employees with evolving skill sets.

3. **Transparent Communication:**
   Communicate transparently about the responsible use of AI and data privacy policies to build trust among employees.

4. **Specialized Upskilling:**
   Collaborate with external educational institutions to offer specialized courses that align with emerging skill requirements.

5. **Feedback Mechanisms:**
   Establish regular feedback mechanisms through surveys, focus groups, or anonymous channels to identify areas for improvement..

6. **Consistent Well-Being Initiatives:**
   Implement consistent well-being initiatives across all teams and locations to ensure a supportive work environment.

7. **Personalized Leadership Development:** Provide personalized leadership development plans, mentorship programs, and continuous feedback loops to address individual differences.

8. **Diversity Audits and Education Programs:**
   Conduct regular diversity audits, implement mentorship programs for underrepresented groups, and foster inclusivity through education and awareness programs. Address setbacks promptly and transparently

Emotional Intelligence Perspective Implementation

1. **Define Emotional Intelligence:**
   Portray emotional intelligence as the heart's compass, guiding leaders through intricate human connections.

2. **Emphasize Emotional Intelligence as Essence, Not Skill:**
   Present emotional intelligence as the essence of effective human connection, crucial for collaboration and relationship building.

3. **Highlight Emotional Intelligence as a Compass for Leadership**:
   Showcase EI as the bedrock of successful leadership, crucial for forward-thinking leaders in understanding emotions.

4. **Encourage Self-Awareness as Foundation**:
   Promote self-awareness as the cornerstone of emotional intelligence, urging leaders to embark on a self-awareness journey.

5. **Embrace Empathy as Heartbeat of Leadership**:
   Embrace Simon Sinek's view on empathy as leadership's heartbeat, crucial for genuine care and understanding.

6. **Position Empathy as Bridge Connecting Leaders and Teams**:
   Illustrate empathy as the bridge linking leaders and teams, nurturing compassion, and understanding beyond the workplace.

7. **Leave an Emotional Imprint with Empathy**:
   Integrate Maya Angelou's insight on empathetic leaders' enduring impact, highlighting the emotional legacy they leave.

8. **Acknowledge Empathy as a Transformative Culture Catalyst**:
   Reinforce empathy's transformative effect on organizational culture, fostering a sense of value and empowerment.

9. **Recognize Self-Awareness as Conductor's Baton**:
   Acknowledge self-awareness as the guide for authentic human connections, akin to a conductor's baton.

10. **Conclude with Wisdom from Aristotle**:
    Close with Aristotle's wisdom, emphasizing self-knowledge as the foundation of wisdom and its relevance in leadership.

RESEARCH RESOURCES

1. Deloitte: Explore "The future of work in technology" for comprehensive insights into the evolving role of AI in the workplace.
   - Future of work (deloitte.com)

2. McKinsey: Access McKinsey's reports on AI and automation to gain a deeper understanding of the transformative impact of AI on business processes
   - What is the future of Generative AI? | McKinsey

3. Gartner: Dive into Gartner's research on AI in customer service to stay updated on the latest trends and innovations reshaping the customer experience.
   - New Research on Intelligent Automation's Role in Productivity Growth | SS&C Blue Prism

4. Forrester: Forrester's reports on AI-driven customer experience offer valuable perspectives on how AI is revolutionizing customer interactions.
   - Build Customer Service Automation | Ada

5. MIT Sloan Management Review: Stay informed on AI and decision-making by exploring insights and research articles in MIT Sloan Management Review.
   - Artificial Intelligence Course | MIT Online Program | GetSmarter

6. Harvard Business Review: Delve into Harvard Business Review for thought-provoking articles on the strategic implications of AI in enhancing decision-making processes.
   - How AI Can Help Leaders Make Better Decisions Under Pressure (hbr.org)

7. World Economic Forum: Refer to the World Economic Forum's guidelines on AI ethics for a comprehensive understanding of ethical considerations in the age of AI.
   - AI ethics: digital natives on protecting future generations | World Economic Forum (weforum.org)

8. AI Now Institute: AI Now Institute's publications provide valuable insights into the societal implications of AI, with a focus on ethical use and implications.
   - AI_Now_2019_Report.pdf (ainowinstitute.org)

9. PwC: PwC's "AI Predictions 2021" is a valuable resource for understanding AI skills in the workforce and predictions for the future.
   - Report: Navigating PWC's five AI predictions for 2021

10. Adobe: Explore Adobe's blog and research for the intersection of AI and creativity, offering insights into how AI augments creative processes.
    - MAX Sneaks highlights several new generative AI capabilities across photo, video, audio, 3D, and design | Adobe Blog

11. MIT Technology Review: Stay updated on the latest developments at the intersection of AI and creativity with articles from MIT Technology Review.
    - What's next for AI | MIT Technology Review

These sources cover a range of topics and perspectives within the broader realm of AI, providing a rich and varied exploration of the subject matter.

D. Pflug

NOTES

1 (https://www.taylorfrancis.com/books/mono/10.1201/9781003187189/ finding-granite-douglas-pflug).
2 www.riseupandexcel.ca.
3 https://brucelee.com/jeet-kune-do.
4 Transactional Leadership Basics (verywellmind.com).
5 How to Be a Great Leader in Science | Scientific American.
6 Evolving Leadership in a Post-COVID World: The Significance of Situational Leadership (kingsleygate.com).
7 Principle Centered Leadership - Stephen R. Covey - Google Books.
8 196.03.extraordinaryleadership.pdf (porchlightbooks.com).
9 Transformational Leadership Theory: Inspire & Motivate (simplypsychology.org).
10 What Is Servant Leadership? A Philosophy for People-First Leadership (shrm.org).
11 Transformational Leadership - Bernard M. Bass, Ronald E. Riggio - Google Books.
12 (PDF) THE EMERGING SIGNIFICANCE OF VALUES BASED LEADERSHIP: A LITERATURE REVIEW (researchgate.net).
13 Leader as coach : strategies for coaching and developing others : Peterson, David B : Free Download, Borrow, and Streaming : Internet Archive.
14 Certificates in Human Resources Management - McMaster Continuing Education.
15 Jim Collins - Concepts - Level 5 Leadership.
16 Jim Collins - Articles - Good to Great.
17 Books – Daniel Goleman.
18 Jeet Kune Do - Bruce Lee Foundation.

Introduction

ELEVATING LEADERSHIP THROUGH INNOVATIVE COMMUNICATION IN 2025 AND BEYOND

Photo credit: Helena Lopez https://unsplash.com/

In the rapidly evolving landscape of leadership, effective communication has appeared as a cornerstone for success. As leaders navigate the complexities of the modern era, the importance of fostering improved two-way communication with clients, bosses, and subordinates cannot be overstated. This promotes thought into innovative strategies that promise to redefine the dynamics of leadership, ensuring a more connected and collaborative future.

Understanding the evolution of communication

Leaders must recognize that communication paradigms have shifted. In an era dominated by digital interactions and virtual connections, the traditional top-down approach is giving way to a more inclusive, dialogue-driven model. Embracing this evolution is fundamental to staying relevant and resonating with diverse stakeholders.

Leveraging technology to bridge gaps

Technological advancements offer a plethora of tools to enhance communication.

Leaders in 2025 and beyond are encouraged to embrace innovative platforms, virtual collaboration spaces, and AI-driven solutions. These technologies not only facilitate seamless communication but also enable leaders to glean valuable insights, fostering a deeper understanding of the needs and expectations of clients, bosses, and subordinates.

Cultivating a culture of open dialogue

Creating an environment where open and honest communication is encouraged is vital. Leaders should actively seek feedback, actively listen, and foster a culture that values diverse perspectives. By dismantling communication barriers, leaders can build trust and strengthen relationships, enhancing the effectiveness of their leadership.

Tailoring communication styles

Recognizing the diverse needs of clients, bosses, and subordinates is pivotal. Leaders should adopt a flexible communication style that resonates with each group. Whether it is presenting data-driven insights for bosses, crafting compelling narratives for clients, or supplying clear guidance for subordinates, tailoring communication ensures messages are not only heard but also understood.

Prioritizing emotional intelligence

Leadership in 2025 and beyond requires a heightened sense of emotional intelligence. Understanding the emotions and motivations of others fosters empathy and strengthens interpersonal connections. By incorporating emotional intelligence into communication, leaders can navigate challenges more effectively and build lasting relationships.

Continuous learning and adaptation

The landscape of communication is ever evolving. Leaders committed to success in 2025 and beyond must embrace a mindset of continuous learning. Staying informed about emerging trends, adapting communication strategies, and honing new skills are essential for staying ahead in an era where innovation is constant.

Conclusion

Innovative communication is not merely a tool; it is the linchpin that holds together the fabric of effective leadership. Leaders who understand the significance of evolving communication strategies in 2025 and beyond are not just pioneers; they are architects of a future where collaboration, understanding, and connection redefine the very essence of leadership. As we navigate this era of unprecedented change, the leaders who prioritize and master innovative communication will undoubtedly shape a more responsive, agile, and successful tomorrow.

> In a world where ideas connect us, communication is the bridge to innovation. Embrace the power of creative dialogue, where every word becomes a catalyst for progress. Break through the conventional, forge new pathways, and let innovative communication be the heartbeat of your journey towards a future of endless possibilities.
>
> —Douglas Pflug

A HISTORY LESSON

Leadership evolution 1980 to 2020

Photo Credit: Clarisse Meyer https://unsplash.com

"In an era marked by visionary disruptors, adaptive organizational structures, and technology-driven strategies, the leadership landscape of the first two decades of the 21st century underwent a profound metamorphosis. As we explore the evolution from 1980 to 2020 in this chapter, we unravel ten facets illuminating the dynamic and multifaceted nature of leadership's transformative journey."

—Douglas Pflug

A change in leadership style is upon us as we move into 2025. Let us work together as progressive-thinking and forward-moving leaders and build the bandwagon together that others will try to jump in 2025 and beyond.

In the dynamic and ever-evolving landscape of business, the first two decades of the 21st century we have witnessed a transformative journey in leadership paradigms. From visionary disruptors challenging traditional norms to organizational structures adapting for agility, and the pivotal role of technology shaping strategies, leaders navigated an era of unprecedented change. In this chapter, we delve into the evolution of leadership from 2000 to 2020, exploring ten distinct facets that encapsulate the multifaceted nature of this transformative period.

The evolution of leadership: 1980 to 2020

Decoding the legacy of 1980s leadership: A comprehensive analysis

INTRODUCTION: A JOURNEY THROUGH TIME—THE 1980S UNVEILED

Embarking on a reminiscent voyage to the 1980s, this chapter unfolds as a testament to a teenager's experience within the vibrant walls of Waterloo Collegiate Institute in Ontario, Canada. Amid the bustling city of Waterloo, the corridors echoed with the dreams and aspirations of youth, unaware that the unfolding leadership practices of that era would weave a narrative casting shadows over our present challenges.

A TAPESTRY OF BOUNDLESS POSSIBILITIES: THE TEENAGER'S PERSPECTIVE

As a teenager navigating the halls, the 1980s appeared as an epoch of boundless possibilities. The world outside, adorned with neon lights, pulsating to iconic music, and abuzz with emerging technologies, painted a canvas of excitement and promise. Little did we grasp then that the leadership practices shaping our environment would sculpt a silhouette that extends into the challenges confronting us today.

THE EPOCH OF TRANSFORMATION: POLICIES THAT RESONATE TODAY

Indeed, the 1980s stand as a pivotal era in global leadership, where transformative policies were set into motion. Policies that, like echoes through time, continue to shape the contours of contemporary challenges. The impact of these policies, however, unfolds as a multidimensional narrative, subject to the diverse perspectives on the performance of leaders during this transformative decade.

NAVIGATING THE INTERCONNECTED WEB: UNRAVELING COMPLEX LANDSCAPES

To comprehend the intricate tapestry of present-day challenges, our journey takes us through the interconnected web of decisions that influenced geopolitical, economic, and societal landscapes. The policies enacted during the 1980s become waypoints, guiding our exploration into their repercussions, and fueling the ongoing debate about their lasting impact on the challenges faced in the 2020s.

RECOGNIZING THE INDELIBLE MARK: NAVIGATING THE LEGACY

As I look back, reflect, and evaluate my journey as a young man navigating the legacy of the 1980s, we confront the indelible mark left by the decisions made during that transformative decade. The interconnectedness of geopolitical, economic, and societal factors emerges as the underlying thread weaving through the complexity of our present challenges. As we gaze into the rearview mirror of the past, we acknowledge our collective role in shaping a future that not only learns from the lessons of yesteryears but also strives toward a more resilient and equitable world.

ECONOMIC POLICIES: TRICKLE-DOWN ECONOMICS AND NEOLIBERALISM

The embrace of neoliberal economic policies, notably "trickle-down economics," characterized the 1980s. Leaders in Western countries, such as President Ronald Reagan and Prime Minister Margaret Thatcher, championed tax cuts for the wealthy, aiming for broader benefits. Critics argue that these policies exacerbated income inequality, contributing to lasting economic disparities.

DEREGULATION: UNLEASHING FINANCIAL MARKETS

Significant financial deregulation, including the dismantling of the Glass-Steagall Act in the United States, defined the 1980s. Some critics contend that this contributed to the conditions that later precipitated the global fiscal crisis in 2008, emphasizing the potential risks associated with unchecked financial markets.

FOREIGN POLICY: COLD WAR TENSIONS AND MILITARIZATION

Heightened Cold War tensions defined the 1980s, marked by an arms race and confrontations. While leaders engaged in dialogue, critics argue that the focus on military buildup and proxy wars had negative consequences, leaving lasting geopolitical challenges.

ENVIRONMENTAL POLICIES: BALANCING INDUSTRY AND ECOLOGY

The 1980s saw limited emphasis on environmental regulations. Policies favoring industry interests over ecological concerns, particularly in the United States, received criticism for their long-term impact on environmental sustainability.

SOCIAL POLICIES: THE HIV/AIDS EPIDEMIC AND DELAYED RESPONSES

The emergence of the HIV/AIDS epidemic in the early 1980s exposed inadequate responses from governments, particularly in the United States. Critics argue that delayed actions contributed to the virus's spread, highlighting shortcomings in public health strategies.

TRADE POLICIES: GLOBALIZATION AND ECONOMIC DISPARITIES

The push for globalization and trade liberalization in the 1980s aimed at boosting economic growth but led to job losses and disparities. Critics highlight the need for balanced trade policies that consider the societal impact of economic shifts.

TECHNOLOGY AND JOB DISPLACEMENT: UNANTICIPATED CONSEQUENCES

The rapid technological advancements in the 1980s contributed to automation and deindustrialization. Critics argue that leaders did not adequately address the societal impact of job displacement, leading to economic dislocation and social challenges.

HEALTHCARE POLICIES: ESCALATING COSTS

The 1980s saw the beginning of rising healthcare costs. Insufficient regulation and market-oriented policies are criticized for contributing to escalating expenses, laying the groundwork for ongoing healthcare challenges.

EDUCATION FUNDING: BUDGET CUTS AND DISPARITIES

Budget cuts in education during the 1980s impacted public school funding, leading to long-term consequences and educational disparities. Critics stress the importance of prioritizing education as a foundation for societal development.

HOUSING POLICIES: DEREGULATION AND MARKET VOLATILITY

Deregulation extended to housing markets in the 1980s, contributing to market volatility. Critics argue that this played a role in subsequent housing crises, emphasizing the need for balanced housing policies.

Conclusion

Assessing the impact of 1980s leadership involves recognizing the complex, interconnected nature of historical events. Perspectives on these policies differ, and the ongoing discourse shapes our understanding of the challenges faced in subsequent decades. By examining these policies holistically, we gain valuable insights into the intricacies of leadership decisions and their far-reaching consequences.

In the transformative period between 1980 to 2020, leadership witnessed a profound metamorphosis, departing from traditional paradigms toward adaptive, inclusive, and forward-thinking models.

Among the trailblazers, Elon Musk, founder of Tesla and SpaceX, stands out for his disruptive approach to industries. Musk's visionary leadership not only propelled electric cars and space exploration to new heights but also challenged conventional business norms.

Another exemplar is Satya Nadella, CEO of Microsoft, who orchestrated a cultural transformation within the company. Under Nadella's guidance, Microsoft shifted from a closed and competitive stance to an open and collaborative one, fostering innovation and adaptability.

Agile organizational structures

The hierarchical structures predominant in the early 2000s faced challenges as organizations embraced a more agile approach. Spotify serves as an emblematic example.

Spotify disrupted the music industry and redefined organizational structures by adopting a "tribe" and "squad" model, facilitating cross-functional collaboration, and enabling quicker decision-making. This departure from rigid hierarchies highlights the necessity for contemporary organizations to foster fluid structures that encourage innovation and responsiveness.

Another notable example is Zappos, an online shoe and clothing retailer, which implemented holacracy—a management philosophy that distributes authority—highlighting the adaptability required for success in the modern business landscape.

Technology as a catalyst for change

The resistance to technological change in the early 2000s gave way to a new era where leaders embraced and leveraged technology for organizational success. The transformation at Apple under the leadership of Tim Cook is emblematic of this shift. Cook steered Apple into the post-Jobs era by capitalizing on technological advancements. The introduction of new products, and services, and a focus on sustainability underscored Apple's commitment to staying at the forefront of the digital age.

Additionally, Jeff Bezos, the founder of Amazon, reshaped the retail landscape by integrating technology into every aspect of the business, from e-commerce to cloud computing.

Inclusive leadership development at Accenture

Leadership development programs evolved from exclusive endeavors to inclusive initiatives, acknowledging the need for diverse perspectives in decision-making. IBM stands out in this regard, actively promoting diversity and inclusion in its leadership programs. By fostering a culture of inclusivity, IBM positioned itself as a champion of diverse talent pipelines, recognizing that a variety of voices at the leadership table drives innovation and success.

Another commendable example is Salesforce, which has been at the forefront of promoting inclusive leadership development through its commitment to equality and diversity.

Remote work and flexibility

The early 2000s' rigid work structures gave way to a more flexible approach, a transformation accelerated by the events of 2020. Companies like Twitter embraced remote work as a permanent model, challenging the conventional notion of a centralized office. Twitter's announcement to allow employees to work from anywhere signals a broader cultural shift toward acknowledging the importance of flexibility in balancing work and personal life, especially in the face of technological advancements that facilitate remote collaboration.

Microsoft, under the leadership of Satya Nadella, has also embraced a flexible work model, recognizing the need for agility and work-life balance in the modern era.

Transformational leadership at Google under Sundar Pichai

As the business landscape evolved from 2000 to 2020, Google underwent a significant transformation under the leadership of Sundar Pichai. The company's shift into Alphabet reflected a strategic move toward becoming a futuristic conglomerate.

Sundar Pichai's leadership emphasized diverse ventures, innovation, and adaptability, highlighting the need for leaders to steer companies toward future-focused and multifaceted approaches.

Inclusive leadership development at Accenture

In the evolving landscape of leadership, Accenture stands out for its commitment to inclusion and diversity initiatives. The company's diversity index is a testament to its initiative-taking approach to leadership development, emphasizing the importance of fostering an inclusive environment for growth and organizational success.

Uber's ethical transformation under Dara Khosrowshahi

The change in leadership at Uber, led by Dara Khosrowshahi, marked a notable shift toward a more ethical and customer-centric approach. Khosrowshahi''s leadership illustrates the necessity for leaders to navigate organizational transformations by focusing on values, ethics, and long-term sustainability.

Embracing open source at Microsoft under Satya Nadella

Satya Nadella"s leadership at Microsoft witnessed a significant embrace of open-source initiatives. Microsoft"s commitment to open-source development reflects a departure from traditional proprietary approaches, highlighting the adaptability required in leadership to align with evolving industry trends.

Crisis management at Airbnb under Brian Chesky

In the face of the unprecedented challenges brought on by the COVID-19 crisis, Airbnb's CEO Brian Chesky demonstrated exceptional crisis management skills. Chesky's communication and decision-making during these challenging times highlight the need for leaders to navigate unforeseen circumstances and prioritize the well-being of both employees and customers.

These ten examples collectively paint a comprehensive picture of the dynamic and multifaceted nature of leadership evolution from 1980 to 2020, highlighting the varied strategies and approaches undertaken by leaders in response to a rapidly changing business landscape.

Out of this research, the idea for this book, *Ironwill 360° Leadership "Moving Forward" Unlock twelve trends shaping personal leadership for 2025 and beyond for forward-thinking leaders* was born.

Research sources

- Forbes—Elon Musk
  - https://www.forbes.com/sites/forbestechcouncil/2018/09/17/why-elon-musk-is-the-worlds-ultimate-disruptor/?sh=2b7d473b3a17
- Harvard Business Review—Satya Nadella
  - https://hbr.org/2015/12/why-microsoft-ceo-satya-nadella-is-so-successful
- Harvard Business Review—Spotify
  - https://hbr.org/2016/07/how-spotify-builds-products
- Forbes—Zappos
  - https://www.forbes.com/sites/forbescoachescouncil/2019/08/01/lessons-in-agility-what-zappos-can-teach-you-about-adapting-your-organization/?sh=41d4e0f240b9
- CNBC—Tim Cook
  - https://www.cnbc.com/2019/04/29/apple-ceo-tim-cook-on-steve-jobs-the-iphone-privacy-and-innovation.html
- Inc.—Jeff Bezos
  - https://www.inc.com/jeff-haden/25-ways-jeff-bezos-changed-lives-forever.html

- IBM—Diversity
  - https://www.ibm.com/ibm/responsibility/diversity/
- Salesforce—Equality
  - https://www.salesforce.com/company/equality/
- CNBC—Twitter
  - https://www.cnbc.com/2020/05/12/twitter-tells-employees-they-can-work-from-home-forever.html
- Microsoft—Hybrid Workplace Strategy
  - https://news.microsoft.com/2020/10/09/microsofts-hybrid-workplace-strategy-what-it-is-and-how-it-will-impact-employees/
- Business Insider—Google's Transformation
  - https://www.businessinsider.com/alphabet-google-parent-company-strategy-morphs-futuristic-conglomerate-2015-9
- Accenture—Inclusion & Diversity
  - https://www.accenture.com/us-en/about/inclusion-diversity-index
- CNBC—Uber CEO Dara Khosrowshahi explains how the company has changed
  - https://www.cnbc.com/2020/09/10/uber-ceo-dara-khosrowshahi-explains-how-the-company-has-changed.html
- Microsoft—Microsoft Open Source
  - https://opensource.microsoft.com/
- Airbnb—A Message from our CEO
  - https://news.airbnb.com/a-message-from-airbnb-co-founder-and-ceo-brian-chesky/

Part I

2025 and Beyond

Photo credit: Braden Cullem https://unsplash.com

As you embark on the path of personal leadership, you're not merely racing towards the future of 2025 and beyond; you're establishing the pace for others, guiding your journey with unwavering determination, resilience, and an enduring commitment to continuous growth for everyone involved. It is time to #RiseUpAndExcel.

—Douglas Pflug

DOI: 10.1201/9781003518099-2

Chapter 1

Digital Mindfulness

**EMBRACING TECHNOLOGY TO ENHANCE
SELF-AWARENESS AND BALANCE IN DAILY LIFE**

Photo Credit: Kid Circus https://unsplash.com/

Mindfulness is the key to unlocking the full potential of technology.
Embrace it with awareness, and let it enhance your life rather than
dominate it.

—Douglas Pflug

DOI: 10.1201/9781003518099-3

MY THOUGHTS AND COMMENTARY

Mindfulness is the key to unlocking the full potential of technology. Embrace it with awareness, and let it enhance your life rather than dominate it.

HOW I DISCOVERED MY LOVE AND DESIRE TO LEARN MORE ABOUT AI

In October 2023, I attended a Blood Spatter Pattern Analysis (BSPA) conference in Baltimore, Maryland, with my wife, Michelle Pflug, who teaches BSPA at the Ontario Police College. Over the years, I have attended similar conferences, and truthfully, when the subject matter experts start speaking, it always reminds me of the sound byte when a teacher speaks in the old *Charlie Brown* cartoons: '*inaudible waa wwaaa.*'[1]

On this particular night, during a social event, I had the pleasure of meeting Philip Joris[2] and Vasiliki (Vanessa) Pasalidi-Chantzi,[3] who were conference attendees and presenters on how they have incorporated their AI sphere of influence in the BSPA world. Let us just say that both amazing individuals have more letters after their respective names than my first, second, and last names combined! HA-HA.

As we chatted for an hour or so, I was amazed that they spoke to me as a peer, but better yet, about the future of AI as they saw it. This sparked my interest in AI in many aspects of life, and, trusting in my research since then, I have read hundreds of articles, journals, news stories, etc., fueling this new passion for knowledge.

> *With that in mind, I recently stumbled upon a mind-blowing article that left me in awe—*
> *"VR in HR: How human resources can use VR and AR technology" by George Lawton (published on December 16, 2021).*[4]

As a seasoned individual with 57 years under my belt, reflecting on over four decades of work experience, I have witnessed the transformation of music storage from record albums to cassettes, then Compact Discs, and now digital files. The evolution in my beloved realm of music, spanning 146 years from its 1877 inception to today's digital files, is nothing short of astonishing.

What strikes me as ironic is that the predicted developments in the article centred around the use of AI align seamlessly with this evolution. While the journey of music storage took a century and a half, the rise of AI, introduced in 1980, has grown exponentially in a mere 43 years, shaping the future as we now know it across every facet of life.

This reflection is nothing short of epic, signifying a monumental shift that will redefine the way we navigate work, life, and recreation, both on a personal and professional level.

The potential implications of VR and AR in HR processes resonate deeply, promising to revolutionize how we recruit, onboard, train, and collaborate in virtual workspaces. It is a testament to the relentless march of technological progress, and I find myself eagerly anticipating the transformative journey ahead.

I have compiled the charts below to prove my point.

Timelines	Music devices
1877	The invention of the Phonograph by Thomas Edison.
1901	First Commercially Produced Record Albums
1948	Introduction of the Long-Playing (LP) Record
1950s	Rise of Vinyl Records
1982	Introduction of Compact Discs (CDs)
1990s	Onward: Digital Distribution
1877–2023	No real developments anticipated: **146 years**. Most anticipated developments stem from the use of AI.

In comparison:

Timelines	Artificial Intelligence (AI)
1956	The term "artificial intelligence" was coined in 1956.
1980s to 1990s	Expert Systems and Commercialization: AI experienced a resurgence, however limitations in technology led to another period of skepticism.
1990s to 2000s	Practical applications of AI, especially in machine learning, gained traction and companies started using AI technologies for tasks like data mining, speech recognition, and image processing. Google, founded in 1998, played a significant role in the integration of machine learning into search algorithms.
2010s	Deep Learning and Big Data marked a significant shift with advances in hardware, the availability of vast datasets, and improved algorithms contributed to breakthroughs and AI technologies became more integrated into consumer products and services.
2010–onward	Mainstream Integration and AI become deeply integrated into various aspects of daily life. Voice-activated assistants, recommendation systems, autonomous vehicles, smart devices, and data analysis and decision-making all leverage AI technologies.

(Continued)

Timelines	Artificial Intelligence (AI)
2023–onward	AI Applications are now an integral part of many industries and technologies. It powers virtual assistants, chatbots, recommendation systems, and autonomous vehicles making it a mainstream technology.
1980–2034	Exponential growth over the **43 years** with no end in sight.

The data for this chart was compiled from Source: www.OpenAi.com ChatGPT 3.5

I am eager to witness the integration of AI for forward-thinking leaders in the constantly evolving landscape of Human Resources (HR).

A profound transformation is taking place, and at its forefront are the immersive technologies of Virtual Reality (VR) and Augmented Reality (AR). George Lawton's insightful exploration in the article "VR in HR: How human resources can use VR and AR technology" sheds light on the potential impact of these technologies on various HR processes, providing a glimpse into a future where recruitment, onboarding, training, and workspaces are redefined.

In my classes on facilitating 'adult conversations' between employers and employees, I consistently emphasize three key points:

1. Document, document, document.
2. Always be prepared and never enter a situation unprepared.
3. Avoid having these meetings when "H.A.L.T" factors (hungry, angry, lonely, or tired) or a combination of them exist, as they can quickly sideline or derail a coaching session.

With that in mind, AI can mitigate some human vulnerabilities like pride, ego, or anger from the equation, enabling more professional, efficient, and better-understood sessions for all parties involved.

A PRACTICAL REVOLUTION

The article emphasizes a change in thinking. In the practicality of VR technology. The affordability of VR hardware has reached a point where organizations, including giants like Accenture and Bank of America, can invest in massive quantities of VR headsets for training purposes. This marks a turning point, making immersive experiences more accessible and scalable than ever before.

THE SYMBIOSIS OF VR AND AR

Lawton underlines the constructive collaboration between VR and AR in reshaping HR processes. While VR immerses individuals in a 3D world, AR overlays information onto the real world, together laying the foundation for the metaverse. This convergence is not just a technological advancement but a catalyst influencing diverse industries.

DYNAMIC TRAINING AND ENGAGEMENT

VR's immersive nature opens avenues for dynamic interactions, creating a unique training environment. High-potential leaders can be exposed to complex business scenarios in a safe and controlled manner, fostering effective learning and development. The article paints a picture where traditional training methods pale in comparison to the engagement and retention achieved through VR.

REVOLUTIONIZING RECRUITMENT

The evolution of recruitment videos finds its zenith in VR. The article suggests that VR offers a more interactive and engaging recruitment experience. Organizations can now present themselves in ways that transcend traditional videos, potentially revolutionizing the recruitment landscape.

SKILLS TESTING THROUGH SIMULATION

VR emerges as a tool for skills testing during recruitment, particularly in high-volume hiring. Simulating job-related scenarios provides a unique and effective way to assess specific skills required for various roles, opening new possibilities for candidate evaluation.

TRANSFORMATIVE ONBOARDING EXPERIENCE

Acknowledging the crucial role of a positive onboarding experience, the article posits VR as a solution. Especially relevant in the post-pandemic era, VR helps create a sense of presence and connection among geographically dispersed employees, fostering trust and professional relationships.

SOFT SKILLS TRAINING IN A NEW DIMENSION

Soft skills training, including diversity, equity, and inclusion (DEI) programs, finds a promising ally in VR. Studies cited in the article suggest that VR-enabled soft skills training is not only more efficient but emotionally engaging, democratizing access to this type of learning.

ADVANCING TECHNICAL TRAINING AND DEVELOPMENT

Industries at the forefront of technological advancements, such as manufacturing, aerospace, and government agencies, are leveraging VR and AR for technical training. The potential to improve workforce efficiency, enhance quality, and reduce errors positions these technologies as indispensable tools.

CRAFTING A CONNECTED FUTURE WORKPLACE

In envisioning the future workplace, VR and AR become solutions to bridge the gap created by geographically dispersed teams. The creation of virtual offices within video conferencing applications aims to provide a sense of togetherness, rekindling the camaraderie lost in remote work settings.

CHALLENGES AND OPPORTUNITIES

While celebrating the potential, the article does not shy away from acknowledging challenges. Ergonomic concerns, especially for older workers, and the need for improved content development and management in immersive experiences stand out as areas ripe for innovation.

CONCLUSION

Lawton's article serves as a comprehensive guide to the transformative potential of VR and AR in HR. As organizations continue to navigate this virtual frontier, the integration of immersive technologies promises to redefine the HR landscape, offering unparalleled opportunities for engagement, learning, and connection.

In the pursuit of revolutionizing HR practices, the journey into the virtual realm is not without challenges. However, as advancements continue and innovations address existing concerns, the future painted by Lawton appears both exciting and full of promise. VR and AR are not just technologies; they are the architects of a new era in Human Resources, where the boundaries between the physical and virtual worlds blur, ushering in a wave of transformative possibilities.

[i] VR in HR: How human resources can use VR and AR technology| TechTarget

INTRODUCTION: THE INTERSECTION OF
MINDFULNESS AND TECHNOLOGY IN LEADERSHIP

The first question that forward thinking leaders must ask is, "What do history and general research illustrate to us?" Let's begin to explore where we were, so that we can plan where we will be mobbing forward.

MINDFUL COMMUNICATION IN THE DIGITAL REALM

Communication lies at the heart of effective leadership, and in the digital realm, the dynamics of interaction have evolved significantly. Mindful communication transcends the superficiality of digital exchanges, fostering genuine connection and understanding. Leaders who embrace mindful communication build trust, inspire collaboration, and navigate the challenges of virtual interactions with grace.

> The most important thing in communication is hearing what isn't said.
> —Peter Drucker

In the landscape of virtual communication, where emails, instant messages, and video calls dominate, the nuances of non-verbal cues and face-to-face interaction often get lost. Mindful communication, however, involves a heightened awareness of the subtleties that define human interaction. It goes beyond the typed words on a screen or the pixels of a video call, delving into the intention behind the message and the emotional context that may not be explicitly expressed.

> The art of communication is the language of leadership.
> —James Humes

Leaders who excel in mindful communication understand the importance of active listening. In a world buzzing with digital noise, the art of truly listening is a rare and invaluable skill. Mindful leaders engage in conversations with a genuine curiosity to understand, rather than merely respond. They create spaces for open dialogue, where team members feel heard, valued, and encouraged to contribute their perspectives.

> The most basic of all human needs is the need to understand and be understood. The best way to understand people is to listen to them.
> —Ralph G. Nichols

Furthermore, mindful communication extends to the written word. In a digital environment saturated with emails and instant messages, leaders who choose their words mindfully create a positive impact. The tone, choice of language, and clarity of communication become crucial elements in conveying messages effectively. Mindful leaders understand that their words have the power to inspire, motivate, or create unnecessary confusion.

> Wise men speak because they have something to say; fools because they have to say something.
>
> —Plato

Navigating the challenges of virtual team meetings, mindful leaders ensure that every participant has an opportunity to express their thoughts. They encourage an inclusive environment where diverse opinions are valued, fostering a sense of belonging among team members. By infusing mindfulness into their communication practices, leaders strengthen the bonds within the team, creating a collaborative atmosphere even in the virtual space.

> The single biggest problem in communication is the illusion that it has taken place.
>
> —George Bernard Shaw

Beyond the formalities of official communication, mindful leaders recognize the importance of informal check-ins. In the absence of physical proximity, a brief, genuine inquiry about the well-being of team members can go a long way in fostering a sense of connection. These small gestures of empathy contribute to a positive team culture, where individuals feel supported not only in their professional endeavors but also in their personal lives.

> To effectively communicate, we must realize that we are all different in the way we perceive the world and use this understanding as a guide to our communication with others.
>
> —Tony Robbins

As leaders adapt to the challenges of the digital realm, the principles of mindful communication become a cornerstone of effective leadership. Mindful leaders recognize that, in the absence of in-person interactions, intentional efforts are needed to build and support strong interpersonal connections. By embracing mindful communication, leaders not only mitigate the pitfalls of virtual interactions but also elevate the overall team dynamics, creating a virtual space where every team member feels valued and heard.

CHALLENGES AND OPPORTUNITIES IN THE INTEGRATION OF MINDFULNESS AND TECHNOLOGY

While the integration of mindfulness and technology offers immense potential for transformative leadership, it is not without its challenges. This will dissect the obstacles that leaders may encounter on this journey and provide insights into overcoming them. From resistance to change within organizational structures to the need for continuous adaptation in the rapidly evolving tech landscape, navigating these challenges requires a nuanced understanding of the intersection between mindfulness and technology.

NAVIGATING RESISTANCE TO CHANGE

One of the primary challenges in integrating mindfulness into the fabric of leadership is resistance to change. Many organizations work within established frameworks and may view mindfulness practices as unconventional or time-consuming.

Leaders advocating for the integration of mindfulness may meet skepticism from team members who are accustomed to traditional approaches.

To address this challenge, leaders need to adopt a strategic and gradual approach. Initiating small, manageable mindfulness practices within teams can serve as an introduction and allow team members to experience the benefits firsthand.

Additionally, leaders should communicate the rationale behind integrating mindfulness, emphasizing its positive impact on individual well-being, team dynamics, and overall organizational success.

> Change is the law of life. And those who look only to the past or the present are certain to miss the future.
> —John F. Kennedy

CONTINUOUS ADAPTATION IN THE TECH LANDSCAPE

The rapid evolution of technology poses another challenge to the integration of mindfulness. New tools, platforms, and communication channels emerge regularly, demanding continuous adaptation.

Leaders may find it challenging to strike a balance between leveraging the latest technological advancements and supporting a mindful approach.

> It is not the strongest of the species that survive, nor the most intelligent, but the one most responsive to change.
> —Charles Darwin

To overcome this challenge, leaders must cultivate a culture of adaptability within their teams. Encouraging a mindset that embraces change and views it as an opportunity rather than a disruption fosters resilience in the face of technological advancements.

Leaders can also set up regular training sessions or workshops to keep their teams updated on the latest technologies while emphasizing the importance of mindful practices to navigate these changes effectively.

> The art of life is a constant readjustment to our surroundings.
>
> —Kakuzo Okakura

QUANTIFYING THE IMPACT OF MINDFULNESS

Measuring the impact of mindfulness practices in a quantifiable manner presents a unique challenge. Traditional performance metrics may not fully capture the holistic benefits of mindfulness on leadership and organizational culture.

Leaders may face skepticism from stakeholders who seek concrete, data-driven evidence of the effectiveness of mindfulness initiatives.

> Not everything that can be counted counts, and not everything that counts can be counted.
>
> —Albert Einstein

To address this challenge, leaders can implement a multifaceted approach to evaluation. While traditional performance metrics are still essential, qualitative assessments, such as employee feedback, surveys, and anecdotal evidence, can supply valuable insights into the impact of mindfulness on team dynamics, collaboration, and overall well-being.

Leaders should communicate these findings transparently to prove the tangible benefits of mindfulness integration.

> The most common way people give up their power is by thinking they don't have any.
>
> —Alice Walker

OPPORTUNITIES ARISING FROM INTEGRATION

Amid the challenges, the integration of mindfulness and technology opens doors to many opportunities for visionary leaders. These opportunities extend beyond individual well-being to encompass organizational resilience, innovation, and a positive workplace culture.

ENHANCED EMPLOYEE WELL-BEING

Mindfulness practices have been consistently linked to improved mental health, reduced stress and increased overall well-being. By prioritizing employee well-being through mindfulness initiatives, leaders create a workplace environment where individuals feel supported, valued, and motivated. This, in turn, contributes to higher job satisfaction, increased productivity, and a reduction in burnout.

The greatest wealth is health.

—Virgil

INCREASED ORGANIZATIONAL RESILIENCE

In an era marked by rapid technological advancements and unforeseen challenges, organizational resilience is a critical asset. Mindful leaders, equipped with the ability to navigate uncertainties calmly and make informed decisions, contribute to the overall resilience of their organizations.

The integration of mindfulness fosters a culture where adaptability and forward-thinking become ingrained, positioning the organization to thrive in dynamic environments.

Amid the chaos, there is also opportunity.

—Sun Tzu

INNOVATION AND CREATIVITY

Mindfulness has been recognized as a catalyst for creativity and innovation. Leaders who embrace mindfulness practices create an atmosphere where team members feel empowered to think creatively, explore novel ideas, and collaborate on innovative solutions.

The integration of mindfulness fuels a culture of continuous learning and adaptability, essential ingredients for staying ahead in competitive landscapes.

Creativity is intelligence having fun.

—Albert Einstein

POSITIVE WORKPLACE CULTURE

The integration of mindfulness and technology offers leaders an opportunity to shape a positive workplace culture.

Mindful leaders prioritize open communication, empathy, and a collaborative spirit. As a result, teams become cohesive, and the overall workplace culture reflects values such as respect, inclusivity and shared purpose. This positive culture, driven by mindfulness, contributes to higher employee engagement and retention.

> Your work is going to fill a large part of your life, and the only way to be truly satisfied is to do what you believe is great work. And the only way to do great work is to love what you do.
>
> —Steve Jobs

In conclusion, while challenges may go with the integration of mindfulness and technology, visionary leaders recognize the abundant opportunities it presents. By navigating resistance with strategic initiatives, fostering adaptability in the face of technological advancements, and quantifying the impact through a comprehensive evaluation approach, leaders can position their organizations for success.

CONCLUSION: PIONEERING THE FUTURE OF LEADERSHIP THROUGH MINDFULNESS AND TECHNOLOGY

The integration of mindfulness and technology is a pioneering approach to leadership in the 21st century. As we expand our understanding of this symbiotic relationship, leaders are empowered to navigate the complexities of the digital era with wisdom and compassion.

> The best way to predict the future is to create it.
>
> —Peter Drucker

By embracing mindfulness, leaders not only unlock the full potential of technology but also foster a leadership style that transcends traditional boundaries.

The journey toward a holistic leadership approach involves continuous learning, adaptation, and a commitment to the well-being of oneself and the entire organizational ecosystem.

> Life is not about finding yourself; it's about creating yourself.
>
> —George Bernard Shaw

As we stand at the intersection of mindfulness and technology, the future of leadership beckons—a future where awareness, intentionality, and human connection drive organizational success.

Through this transformative journey, leaders become architects of change, shaping a landscape where mindfulness and technology coalesce to create a harmonious and thriving workplace.

The only limit to our realization of tomorrow will be our doubts of today.
—Franklin D. Roosevelt

CHAPTER "TO-DO" CHECKLIST

1. **Acknowledge the Digital Integration:**
   Recognize the integral role of technology in modern leadership.

2. **Embrace Mindfulness as a Key:**
   Understand mindfulness as essential for unlocking technology's full potential in leadership.

3. **Set the Tone with Awareness:**
   Begin the leadership journey with awareness of the digital landscape.

4. **Connect with Steve Jobs' Philosophy:**
   Recognize technology as a tool that amplifies human potential when combined with faith in people.

5. **Embrace Technology with Intention:**
   Understand the importance of intentional engagement with technology.

6. **Integrate Technology Mindfully:**
   Ensure technology serves the greater purpose of human well-being and progress.

7. **Create Digital Boundaries Strategically:**
   Internalize the need for strategic disconnection to foster creativity and innovation.

8. **Simplify with Albert Einstein's Wisdom:**
   Embrace simplicity amid digital clutter to focus on essential matters.

9. **Navigate the Complexities of Digital Leadership:**
   Practice mindful decision-making as a cornerstone of effective leadership.

10. **Foster Innovation through Mindful Leadership:**
    Use mindfulness to inspire creativity and adaptability within organizations.

FINAL THOUGHTS

"Navigating the digital frontier: Leaders trained in digital mindfulness"
In the era beyond 2025, leadership training must equip leaders with the skills of digital mindfulness. Leaders who master the art of mindful engagement with technology not only enhance their focus and productivity but also foster a culture of digital well-being within their teams. Through training, leaders learn to strike a balance between leveraging digital tools for efficiency and preserving mental clarity, ensuring that the digital landscape becomes a realm of opportunities rather than distractions.

"Mindful leadership in the digital age: Training tomorrow's leaders"
Leadership training for 2025 and beyond is a journey into mindful leadership. In a world inundated with digital noise, effective leaders are those who can navigate the complexities of technology while maintaining mental balance. Training programs should instill practices that cultivate awareness, attention, and intention in the digital space. Tomorrow's leaders will thrive by leading with a mindful approach and making strategic decisions while preserving their well-being and that of their teams.

These messages emphasize the importance of incorporating digital mindfulness into leadership training, recognizing its significance in enhancing focus, decision-making, and overall well-being in the digital age.

CHAPTER QUOTES

1. Ralph G. Nichols

> The most basic of all human needs is the need to understand and be understood. The best way to understand people is to listen to them.
> https://www.goodreads.com/quotes/167082-the-most-basic-of-all-human-needs-is-the-need

2. James Humes

The art of communication is the language of leadership.
https://www.forbes.com/sites/jimpaymar/2012/02/02/
speak-like-a-leader/?sh=5f483ce67144

3. Kakuzo Okakura

The art of life is a constant readjustment to our surroundings.
https://priscillaajacks.wordpress.com/2016/02/10/the-art-of-
life-is-a-constant-readjustment-to-our-surroundings-
kakuzo-okakura/

4. Peter Drucker

The best way to predict the future is to create it.
https://www.brainyquote.com/quotes/peter_drucker_131600

5. Virgil

The greatest wealth is health.
https://www.goodreads.com/
quotes/28440-the-greatest-wealth-is-health

6. Alice Walker

The most common way people give up their power is by thinking
they don't have any.
https://www.brainyquote.com/quotes/alice_walker_385241

7. Franklin D. Roosevelt

The only limit to our realization of tomorrow will be our doubts of
today.
https://www.brainyquote.com/quotes/franklin_d_
roosevelt_164056

8. George Bernard Shaw

The single biggest problem in communication is the illusion that it
has taken place.
https://www.brainyquote.com/quotes/george_
bernard_shaw_385438

9. Tony Robbins

To effectively communicate, we must realize that we are all different
in the way we perceive the world and use this understanding as a
guide to our communication with others.
https://www.inc.com/marcel-schwantes/heres-tony-robbins-
advice-on-how-to-dramatically-improve-your-
communication-skills.html

10. Plato

Wise men speak because they have something to say; fools because they have to say something.

https://www.quora.com/%E2%80%9CWise-men-speak-because-they-have-something-to-say-fools-because-they-have-to-say-something-%E2%80%9D-Agree

11. **Steve Jobs**

Your work is going to fill a large part of your life, and the only way to be truly satisfied is to do what you believe is great work. And the only way to do great work is to love what you do.

https://www.brainyquote.com/quotes/steve_jobs_416859

Mindfulness is the key to unlocking the full potential of technology. Embrace it with awareness, and let it enhance your life rather than dominate it.

—Douglas Pflug

NOTES

1 Charlie Brown Teacher Speaking - YouTube.
2 (7) Philip Joris | LinkedIn.
3 (7) Vasiliki (Vanessa) Pasalidi-Chantzi | LinkedIn.
4 VR in HR: How human resources can use VR and AR technology | TechTarget.

Chapter 2

Holistic Well-Being

**INTEGRATING MENTAL, PHYSICAL, AND EMOTIONAL
HEALTH FOR A MORE COMPREHENSIVE APPROACH
TO PERSONAL FULFILLMENT**

Photo Credit: Justin Veenema https://unsplash.com/

Holistic well-being is the art of intertwining mental clarity, physical vitality, and emotional resilience, fostering a harmonious symphony that leads to a more fulfilling and balanced life journey.

—Douglas Pflug

DOI: 10.1201/9781003518099-4

MY THOUGHTS AND COMMENTARY

Holistic well-being is the art of intertwining mental clarity, physical vitality, and emotional resilience, fostering a harmonious symphony that leads to a more fulfilling and balanced life journey.

As a 58-year-old baby boomer, I recognize the need for continuous improvement and positive changes in both my professional and personal life, especially as retirement approaches. Understanding the importance of holistic well-being, which involves mental clarity, physical vitality, and emotional resilience, I am committed to fostering a harmonious balance. This mindset enhances my overall well-being and contributes to a positive work environment, aligning with the evolving needs of both the workplace and home.

The leaders of the baby boomer era got us to this point, and I hope that this book fills the void for the question "What's next?"

CONSIDERATIONS FOR ACHIEVING A HOLISTIC APPROACH

Lifelong learning and skill development

- Embrace continuous learning by staying informed about industry trends, innovative technologies, and best practices.
- Actively seek professional development opportunities to enhance skills and adapt to the evolving demands of the workplace.

Integrating technology in work and life

- Embrace technology for improved efficiency and communication, both at work and in personal life.
- Explore digital tools and platforms that facilitate work-life balance, such as scheduling apps, virtual collaboration tools, and mindfulness apps.

Prioritize mental and emotional well-being

- Incorporate mindfulness practices like meditation or deep breathing exercises for mental clarity and emotional resilience.
- Cultivate emotional intelligence by fostering self-awareness and empathy in professional and personal interactions.

Balancing work and personal life

- Set clear boundaries between work and personal life to maintain a healthy balance.
- Prioritize self-care by scheduling regular breaks, vacations, and activities that bring joy and relaxation outside of work responsibilities.

Promoting a positive work environment

- Foster a positive and inclusive workplace culture by promoting team-work, open communication, and mutual support among colleagues.
- Encourage a healthy work-life balance for yourself and your team, recognizing the importance of well-being in overall job satisfaction and productivity.

By implementing these strategies, you can contribute to an integrated approach in both your professional and personal life, fostering well-being, balance, and adaptability in the ever-evolving landscape of work and home.

I UTILIZE FIVE TIPS TO ASSIST IN ORIENTING MYSELF IN THE MULTIGENERATIONAL WORKFORCE

As a baby boomer leadership instructor, I always get asked how we enhance collaboration in the evolving workplace with Millennials, Gen X, Y, and Z. To better navigate this dynamic landscape, particularly as we evolve as leaders, consider these key strategies:

Embrace diversity and inclusion

- Appreciate diverse perspectives and work styles across different generations.
- Cultivate an inclusive environment that values contributions from individuals of all ages.

Adopt a growth mindset

- Welcome the latest ideas, technologies, and work approaches with an open mindset.
- Stay receptive to learning from younger colleagues and adapting to evolving workplace dynamics.

Improve technology skills

- Stay abreast of industry technology trends.
- Enhance technological proficiency through training or mentorship, facilitating smoother collaboration with younger generations.
- Do not be that guy who says, *"I'm my generation..."* or *"We've never done it that way before"*. These responses even anger me, a baby boomer!

Mentorship and reverse mentoring

- Share your experience through mentorship with younger colleagues.
- Embrace reverse mentoring, learning from younger team members about emerging trends and innovative perspectives.

Effective communication

- Adapt to various communication styles preferred by different generations.
- Foster transparent communication to ensure information flows seamlessly across the team.

By implementing these strategies, you can effectively navigate the challenges and opportunities of collaborating with individuals from diverse generations as you evolve as a progressive-thinking and forward-moving leader.

Always remember that leadership is about generating, mentoring, and supporting the followers you cultivate.

Resource: The book _Generations at Work Generations at Work: Managing the Clash of Boomers, Gen Xers, and Gen Years in the Workplace_: Zemke, Ron, Raines, Claire, Filipczak, Bob: 9780814432334: Books Amazon.ca

WHAT DO HISTORY AND GENERAL RESEARCH ILLUSTRATE TO US?

Introduction: The essence of holistic leadership in a dynamic world

In the ever-evolving landscape of leadership in 2025 and beyond, the importance of holistic well-being becomes increasingly clear. This promotes thought into the multifaceted nature of well-being, emphasizing the interconnectedness of mental clarity, physical vitality, and emotional resilience. Leaders are encouraged to view well-being not as a singular pursuit but as a harmonious symphony that enriches their personal and professional journey.

Holistic well-being is not just a distant melody in the orchestra of leadership; it is the underlying rhythm that propels leaders toward fulfillment and balance. This rhythm influences not only their personal lives but also the culture and success of the organizations they lead.

The introduction sets up holistic well-being as an integral aspect of leadership, portraying it as a harmonious rhythm that goes beyond individual well-being, shaping organizational culture and success.

NURTURING MENTAL CLARITY: CULTIVATING FOCUS IN THE AGE OF DISTRACTION

> The ability to concentrate and to use your time well is everything if you want to succeed in business—or almost anywhere else.
>
> —Lee Iacocca

Lee Iacocca's wisdom sets the stage for exploring the first movement in the symphony of holistic well-being: nurturing mental clarity.

This promotes thought into the challenges leaders face in supporting focus in an era filled with distractions.

Leaders are encouraged to cultivate mental clarity as a foundation for effective decision-making, innovation, and sustained success.

Lee Iacocca's perspective resonates—nurturing mental clarity is not a luxury but a prerequisite for success, enabling leaders to navigate the complexities of leadership with focus and decisiveness.

Effective leadership demands a disciplined mind capable of discerning essential tasks amid the cacophony of information. Leaders must not only focus on what to do but also develop the discernment to drop distractions and prioritize what truly matters.

As leaders nurture mental clarity, the words of Steve Jobs become a guiding principle—innovation is saying no to a thousand things. Mental clarity involves not just focusing on what to do but also having the discernment to drop distractions and prioritize what truly matters.

The conclusion reinforces the importance of mental clarity by aligning with Steve Jobs' perspective on innovation and the art of discernment in leadership.

FOSTERING PHYSICAL VITALITY: THE KEYSTONE OF SUSTAINABLE LEADERSHIP

> Take care of your body. It's the only place you have to live.
>
> —Jim Rohn

Jim Rohn's insight becomes the central theme in exploring the second movement of holistic well-being: fostering physical vitality.

This underscores the significance of physical health in sustaining effective leadership.

Leaders are encouraged to prioritize self-care, recognizing that physical vitality is not only a personal responsibility but a keystone for sustainable leadership.

In progressive thinking and forward-moving leadership, Jim Rohn's words echo—the importance of fostering physical vitality is not just about personal well-being but about creating a foundation for enduring leadership that positively influences organizational culture and success.

Leadership longevity is not merely about climbing the ladder of success; it is about the satisfaction derived from the journey itself. Fostering physical vitality is not just about extending life but enhancing the quality of the leadership journey.

As leaders foster physical vitality, the words of Arianna Huffington become a guiding light—success is not about climbing up the ladder but about how satisfying the journey is. Fostering physical vitality is not just about longevity; it is about enhancing the quality of the leadership journey.

The conclusion emphasizes the quality of the leadership journey, aligning with Arianna Huffington's perspective on the satisfaction derived from success and the importance of fostering physical vitality.

CULTIVATING EMOTIONAL RESILIENCE: THE HEARTBEAT OF EFFECTIVE LEADERSHIP

> It's not the load that breaks you down; it's the way you carry it.
> —Lou Holtz

Lou Holtz's perspective becomes the focal point in exploring the third movement of holistic well-being: cultivating emotional resilience.

This promotes thought into the challenges leaders face in navigating the emotional complexities of leadership.

Leaders are encouraged to view emotional resilience not as immunity to stress but as the ability to carry the load with grace and adaptability.

In progressive thinking and forward-moving leadership, Lou Holtz's wisdom resonates—cultivating emotional resilience is not about avoiding challenges but about developing the strength to carry the emotional load with composure and adaptability.

Leaders are called to develop emotional resilience, the strength to carry emotional loads with composure and adaptability. It challenges the notion of avoiding challenges and instead encourages leaders to navigate them with strength and poise.

As leaders cultivate emotional resilience, the words of Brené Brown become a guiding principle—vulnerability is not winning or losing; it is having the courage to show up and be seen. Cultivating emotional resilience involves embracing vulnerability, fostering authentic connections, and leading with empathy.

The conclusion emphasizes the courage to show up and be seen, aligning with Brené Brown's perspective on vulnerability and its role in cultivating emotional resilience.

CONCLUSION: THE HARMONIOUS SYMPHONY OF LEADERSHIP WELL-BEING

In conclusion, holistic well-being is the symphony that underscores effective leadership in 2025 and beyond. The interconnected movements of nurturing mental clarity, fostering physical vitality, and cultivating emotional resilience create a harmonious rhythm that enriches the lives of leaders and reverberates throughout their organizations.

As leaders embrace the art of intertwining these elements, they not only enhance their well-being but also contribute to a culture of balance, fulfillment, and sustained success. In the dynamic landscape of leadership, the symphony of holistic well-being is not just a personal pursuit; it is the key to orchestrating a legacy of resilience, vitality, and genuine leadership impact.

The conclusion reinforces the idea of well-being as a symphony that enriches the lives of leaders and organizations. It underscores the interconnected movements and their role in creating a culture of balance, fulfillment, and sustained success. The symphony of holistic well-being is positioned as a key element in orchestrating a legacy of resilience, vitality, and genuine leadership impact.

THE EMPHASIS ON HOLISTIC WELL-BEING IN LEADERSHIP

The emphasis on holistic well-being in leadership, especially in the evolving landscape of 2025 and beyond, is of paramount importance for several reasons:

INTERCONNECTED NATURE OF WELL-BEING

The introduction highlights that well-being extends beyond a singular dimension, incorporating mental clarity, physical vitality, and emotional resilience. Recognizing the interconnectedness of these aspects paints a holistic picture of well-being, acknowledging that neglecting one area can impact others.

This understanding promotes a more comprehensive approach to leadership and personal development.

FOUNDATIONAL ROLE IN LEADERSHIP

Describing well-being as the underlying rhythm that propels leaders toward fulfillment and balance emphasizes its foundational role. It suggests that an individual's well-being serves as the cornerstone for effective leadership, influencing not only personal lives but also organizational culture and success.

By establishing well-being as a fundamental aspect, the introduction positions it as a catalyst for overall leadership effectiveness.

CULTURAL IMPACT

The idea that well-being influences the culture of organizations reinforces its significance. The introduction implies that a leader's well-being sets the tone for the well-being culture within the organization.

Leaders who prioritize holistic well-being are likely to foster a workplace environment that values the health and satisfaction of its members. This, in turn, can contribute to increased productivity, creativity, and employee satisfaction.

LONG-TERM LEADERSHIP SUSTAINABILITY

The subsequent sections on nurturing mental clarity, fostering physical vitality, and cultivating emotional resilience delve into specific components of well-being. These components are not only essential for immediate effectiveness but also contribute to long-term leadership sustainability.

Focusing on mental clarity, physical health, and emotional resilience equips leaders with the tools necessary to navigate challenges over an extended period, promoting enduring success.

WISDOM FROM DIVERSE PERSPECTIVES

Introducing quotes from various thought leaders like Lee Iacocca, Jim Rohn, and Lou Holtz adds depth to the discussion.

Drawing on the wisdom of these figures underscores that the importance of well-being is not a new or trendy concept; it is a timeless principle recognized by leaders across different fields and eras. This lends credibility to the argument and positions well-being as a universal and enduring aspect of effective leadership.

SYMPHONIC METAPHOR

The metaphor of a symphony in the conclusion adds a layer of elegance to the discussion.

Describing well-being as a harmonious rhythm and interconnected movements as the elements of this symphony paints a vivid and memorable image. This metaphor reinforces the idea that well-being is not just a checklist of individual tasks but a harmonious integration of mental, physical, and emotional elements, contributing to a holistic and impactful leadership journey.

In summary, the importance of holistic well-being in leadership is highlighted through its interconnected nature, foundational role, cultural impact, long-term sustainability, wisdom from diverse perspectives, and the metaphor of a symphony.

These elements collectively make a compelling case for well-being as an integral and enduring aspect of effective leadership in the contemporary and future landscape.

CHAPTER "TO-DO" CHECKLIST

1. **Embrace Self-Awareness:**
   Foster a deep understanding of oneself, including strengths, weaknesses, and values, to lead authentically.

2. **Prioritize Work-Life Balance:**
   Recognize the importance of maintaining harmony between professional responsibilities and personal well-being to sustain long-term success.

3. **Promote Physical Wellness:**
   Encourage regular exercise, proper nutrition, and adequate rest to optimize physical health and energy levels.

4. **Nurture Emotional Intelligence:**
   Develop the ability to recognize, understand, and manage emotions in oneself and others to foster healthy relationships and effective communication.

5. **Cultivate Mental Resilience:**
   Build coping mechanisms and stress management techniques to navigate challenges with clarity and composure.

6. **Foster Social Connection:**
   Create opportunities for meaningful connections and support networks among team members to enhance collaboration and morale.

7. **Encourage Lifelong Learning:**
   Embrace a growth mindset and encourage continuous learning and development to adapt to evolving challenges and opportunities.

8. **Practice Mindfulness:**
Incorporate mindfulness practices such as meditation and reflection to cultivate present-moment awareness and reduce stress.

9. **Support Financial Wellness:**
Provide resources and education to support financial stability and reduce financial stress among team members.

10. **Champion a Purpose-Driven Culture:**
Align organizational goals with meaningful values and a sense of purpose to inspire motivation, resilience, and fulfillment among employees.

FINAL THOUGHTS

Holistic Well-Being

- Embrace Holistic Well-Being as a Cornerstone of Leadership Beyond 2025:
  In the evolving landscape of leadership, success will be defined not only by financial achievements but by the holistic well-being of individuals and teams. Leaders must recognize that fostering mental, emotional, and physical health is integral to organizational prosperity. Beyond 2025, prioritize a culture that values work-life balance, mental resilience, and personal growth. By placing holistic well-being at the core of leadership, organizations can unleash the full potential of their teams, creating a sustainable and thriving future.

- Lead with Empathy and Purpose for Sustainable Well-Being:
  Looking forward, leadership's success hinges on the ability to lead with empathy and purpose. Beyond 2025, cultivate a workplace environment that prioritizes the emotional and mental health of team members. Leaders should actively seek to understand the unique challenges their teams face and provide support that goes beyond traditional professional development. By aligning organizational goals with a genuine

commitment to the well-being of individuals, leaders can foster a culture of purpose, resilience, and sustainable success in the years to come.

CHAPTER QUOTES

1. Lou Holtz

It's not the load that breaks you down; it's the way you carry it.
https://www.brainyquote.com/quotes/lou_holtz_120090

2. Lee Iacocca

The ability to concentrate and to use your time well is everything if you want to succeed in business—or almost anywhere else.
https://www.goodreads.com/quotes/7910547-the-ability-to-concentrate-and-to-use-your-time-well

3. Jim Rohn

Take care of your body. It's the only place you have to live.
https://www.success.com/quotations-take-care-of-your-body/

4. Arianna Huffington

Success is not about climbing up the ladder but about how satisfying the journey is.
https://www.inc.com/jessica-stillman/6-quotes-to-make-you-rethink-what-success-means.html

5. Brené Brown

Vulnerability is not winning or losing; it is having the courage to show up and be seen.
https://www.goodreads.com/quotes/419079-vulnerability-is-not-winning-or-losing-it-s-having-the

6. Steve Jobs

Innovation is saying no to a thousand things.
https://www.entrepreneur.com/article/244924

Holistic well-being is the art of intertwining mental clarity, physical vitality, and emotional resilience, fostering a harmonious symphony that leads to a more fulfilling and balanced life journey.

Chapter 3

Purpose-Driven Leadership

I AM PRIORITIZING VALUES AND SOCIAL IMPACT TO INSPIRE PURPOSE-DRIVEN DECISION-MAKING

Photo Credit: Alex Azabache https://unsplash.com/

Purpose-driven leadership illuminates the path forward, where values become the compass, and social impact is the destination. In each decision, leaders sculpt a legacy that echoes not only success but a profound sense of purpose, leaving an indelible mark on both the organization and the world.

—Douglas Pflug

DOI: 10.1201/9781003518099-5

MY THOUGHTS AND COMMENTARY

Purpose-driven leadership illuminates the path forward, where values become the compass, and social impact is the destination. In each decision, leaders sculpt a legacy that echoes not only success but a profound sense of purpose, leaving an indelible mark on both the organization and the world.

I consider myself incredibly fortunate to have been surrounded by remarkable parents, friends, and family who consistently supported my journey toward personal growth.

Throughout my life, I have always been a dreamer, but for me, dreams are not mere fantasies; they are the untapped reservoir of ideas waiting to be explored. Unlike idle daydreaming, I passionately believe in transforming these aspirations into tangible goals and then meticulously crafting a plan to bring them to fruition.

At the very core of my ambitious pursuits lie the four cornerstones of my personal leadership philosophy: honor, integrity, passion, and accountability.

These principles form the bedrock of my dreams, propelling me forward on an ever-evolving journey of self-improvement. I perceive purpose-driven leadership as an unwavering guiding light, illuminating the path ahead, with my values acting as a compass and the pursuit of positive social impact serving as my ultimate destination.

In my approach to life and leadership, I am dedicated to embodying purpose-driven principles. Each decision becomes an opportunity to carve out a lasting legacy, extending beyond the realm of personal success to encompass a profound sense of purpose.

This legacy is intended to leave an indelible mark not only on the organizations I engage with but also on the broader world. Through purpose-driven leadership, I aim to contribute meaningfully, making a positive impact that ripples beyond individual accomplishments to benefit the greater community.

Now, let us investigate four key take-a-ways in which the values of honor, integrity, passion, and accountability can contribute to a well-balanced and forward-thinking approach as a purpose-driven leader in both personal and professional spheres:

BUILDING TRUST AND CREDIBILITY

- Upholding a keen sense of honor and integrity establishes trust in all interactions, aligning your actions with your values and fostering credibility both personally and professionally.

- Demonstrating accountability for your decisions and actions reinforces trust, enhancing your reputation as a reliable and trustworthy leader.

INSPIRING OTHERS THROUGH PASSION

- Infusing passion into your endeavors not only motivates you but also serves as a source of inspiration for those around you.
- A leader driven by passion is more likely to create an enthusiastic and dynamic work environment, encouraging others to share in the excitement and commitment to a common purpose.

STRATEGIC DECISION-MAKING

- Operating with integrity in decision-making ensures that choices align with ethical standards and values, contributing to the long-term success of your initiatives.
- Honoring commitments and staying true to your values guides strategic decision-making, fostering a sense of stability and reliability crucial for a purpose-driven leader.

MAINTAINING A HOLISTIC PERSPECTIVE

- Accountability extends beyond professional commitments to include personal ones, recognizing the interconnectedness of personal and professional life.
- Honoring personal values ensures that actions are aligned with an overarching sense of purpose, contributing to a balanced life, and preventing potential conflicts between personal and professional goals.

By seamlessly integrating honor, integrity, passion, and accountability into your leadership approach, you cultivate a well-rounded and forward-thinking mindset. This not only fuels personal development but also enhances your ability to lead with purpose, creating a positive impact in both your personal and professional endeavors.

WHAT TO EXPECT FOR THE BASE LEVEL OF "GOOD" LEADERSHIP

Leadership is a complex and multifaceted concept that encompasses the ability to influence, guide, and inspire individuals or groups toward the achievement of a common goal or vision. It involves a combination of skills, traits, behaviors, and qualities that contribute to effective direction and management.

Leadership is not confined to a specific role or position; individuals at various levels within an organization, community, or society can demonstrate leadership.

FORWARD-THINKING LEADERS—KEY COMPONENTS

Vision

Leaders often have an unobstructed vision of the future and articulate this vision in a way that inspires and motivates others. A compelling vision provides a sense of direction and purpose.

Influence

Leadership involves the ability to influence and persuade others to willingly follow a particular course of action. This influence can be based on a leader's expertise, credibility, or charisma.

Communication

Effective communication is essential for leadership. Leaders must convey their vision, expectations, and ideas clearly and in a manner that resonates with their audience.

Decision-making

Leaders are responsible for making decisions that impact the group or organization. The ability to make well-informed, timely, and ethical decisions is a critical leadership skill.

Adaptability

Leaders need to be adaptable and flexible, especially in dynamic and changing environments. The capacity to navigate uncertainties and lead through change is a hallmark of effective leadership.

Empathy

Empathy involves understanding and considering the feelings, perspectives, and needs of others. Leaders who demonstrate empathy build strong relationships and create a positive organizational culture.

Integrity

Leaders are expected to uphold high ethical standards and demonstrate integrity. Trust is the foundation of effective leadership, and maintaining honesty and transparency is crucial.

Motivation

Leaders inspire and motivate individuals or teams to achieve their best. This may involve recognizing and rewarding accomplishments, providing constructive feedback, and fostering a positive work environment.

Delegation

Effective leaders know how to delegate tasks and responsibilities, recognizing the strengths of their team members. Delegation allows leaders to focus on strategic issues while empowering others to contribute.

Conflict resolution

Leadership involves addressing conflicts and disputes constructively. Leaders should be skilled in managing interpersonal conflicts and fostering a collaborative work environment.

Strategic thinking

Leaders often engage in strategic thinking, considering the long-term goals and objectives of the organization. They make decisions that align with the overall strategy and vision.

Continuous learning

Leadership is a continuous learning journey. Leaders should be open to acquiring new knowledge, skills, and perspectives to adapt to changing circumstances.

Leadership is contextual and can manifest in various settings, including business, politics, education, and community organizations. Different leadership styles exist, ranging from authoritative to participative, and the most effective leaders often adapt their approach to suit the needs of the situation and the people they lead.

In the evolving landscape of leadership, the concept of purpose-driven leadership emerges as a guiding light, illuminating the way for leaders in 2025 and beyond.

This promotes thought into the transformative power of purpose, where values serve as the compass, and social impact becomes the ultimate destination. Every decision made by purpose-driven leaders becomes a brushstroke, contributing to a legacy that transcends mere success, leaving an enduring imprint on the organization and the world.

WHAT DO HISTORY AND GENERAL RESEARCH ILLUSTRATE TO US?

In the evolving landscape of leadership, the concept of purpose-driven leadership emerges as a guiding light, illuminating the way for leaders in 2025 and beyond.

This encourages contemplation on the transformative potential of purpose, with values acting as the guiding force and societal influence emerging as the paramount goal. Each choice undertaken by leaders propelled by purpose becomes a stroke on the canvas, adding to a heritage that goes beyond simple achievement, imprinting a lasting mark on both the entity and the global community.

In progressive thinking and forward-moving leadership, purpose-driven leadership is not a strategy; it is a philosophy—a luminous beacon that draws individuals and organizations toward a meaningful and impactful journey.

The introduction frames purpose-driven leadership as more than just a strategy; it presents it as a guiding philosophy that permeates every aspect of organizational decision-making and culture. Purpose-driven leadership emphasizes aligning actions and decisions with a broader mission or cause, rather than viewing it solely as a tactical approach to achieving short-term goals. This philosophy encourages leaders to prioritize values, ethics, and long-term sustainability, fostering a deeper connection between the organization's objectives and its impact on stakeholders and society at large.

THE ESSENCE OF PURPOSE: VALUES AS THE COMPASS

> Success is not final, failure is not fatal: It is the courage to continue that count.
>
> —Winston Churchill

Winston Churchill's perspective becomes a cornerstone in understanding the essence of purpose-driven leadership.

This explores how purpose, like a compass, guides leaders through challenges and triumphs.

This encourages leaders to infuse their decisions with the courage to align with their values, understanding that true success lies not just in achievements but in the alignment of actions with purpose.

In progressive thinking and forward-moving leadership, Winston Churchill's wisdom echoes—the compass of purpose steers leaders through the complexities of decision-making, ensuring that every action reflects the core values that define the organization.

This emphasizes the role of purpose as a guiding compass that ensures decisions align with the core values of the organization, reinforcing the idea that true success is intertwined with purpose.

As leaders embed purpose into their decisions, Maya Angelou's insight becomes a guiding principle—you cannot use up creativity. Purpose-driven leadership fuels a continuous wellspring of creativity, as leaders navigate challenges with innovative solutions grounded in their organizational values.

Maya Angelou's wisdom reinforces the idea that purpose-driven decisions fuel creativity, creating a continuous wellspring of innovative solutions rooted in organizational values.

SOCIAL IMPACT AS THE DESTINATION: SCULPTING A PROFOUND LEGACY

> The best way to predict the future is to create it.
>
> —Peter Drucker

Peter Drucker's foresight becomes the focal point in this section, emphasizing the initiative-taking nature of purpose-driven leadership.

This explores how purpose-driven leaders not only respond to the present but actively shape the future.

Leaders are encouraged to view social impact not as a byproduct but as the intentional destination of their leadership journey, sculpting a legacy that transcends individual achievements.

In progressive thinking and forward-moving leadership, Peter Drucker's words resonate—social impact is not a consequence of success; it is the intentional outcome of purpose-driven decisions that shape a legacy beyond the organizational realm.

This positions social impact as the intentional outcome of purpose-driven decisions, underscoring the idea that purpose-driven leaders actively shape a legacy that goes beyond organizational success.

As leaders craft a legacy through purpose-driven decisions, Mahatma Gandhi's insight becomes a guiding light—you must be the change you want to see in the world. Purpose-driven leadership inspires leaders to be initiative-taking architects of positive change, leaving an indelible mark on both their organization and the broader societal landscape.

Mahatma Gandhi's wisdom emphasizes that purpose-driven leaders are initiative-taking architects of positive change, aligning with the philosophy of purpose-driven leadership to be the change they wish to see in the world.

CONCLUSION: THE ILLUMINATED LEGACY OF PURPOSE-DRIVEN LEADERSHIP

In conclusion, purpose-driven leadership emerges as a transformative force, illuminating the path forward in the complex and dynamic landscape of leadership in 2025 and beyond.

The compass of values guides leaders through decision-making, ensuring alignment with the organization's core principles. Social impact becomes the intentional destination, shaping a legacy that transcends success and echoes a profound sense of purpose.

As leaders embrace purpose-driven decisions, they not only navigate the challenges of today but become architects of a better and more meaningful tomorrow. In this progressive thinking and forward-moving leadership, purpose-driven leadership is not just a strategy; it is the radiant force that propels leaders toward a legacy of purpose, impact, and enduring success.

The conclusion reinforces the transformative nature of purpose-driven leadership, positioning it as a radiant force that propels leaders toward a legacy marked by purpose, impact, and enduring success. It echoes the philosophy that purpose-driven leaders actively shape a future that goes beyond individual achievements, leaving a lasting imprint on both the organization and the world.

In the ever-evolving landscape of leadership, the concept of purpose-driven leadership emerges as a luminous guiding light, illuminating the way for leaders as they navigate the challenges and opportunities that define the year 2025 and beyond.

This philosophy transcends the conventional strategies of leadership, positioning itself as a transformative force that shapes both individual journeys and organizational destinies.

THE TRANSFORMATIVE POWER OF PURPOSE: NAVIGATING BY VALUES

Winston Churchill's wisdom, "Success is not final, failure is not fatal: It is the courage to continue that counts," resonates as a cornerstone in understanding the essence of purpose-driven leadership. Purpose, akin to a compass, guides leaders through the intricacies of challenges and triumphs, providing direction and clarity in decision-making.

The philosophy encourages leaders to infuse their decisions with the courage to align with their values. It underscores that true success lies not just in accomplishments but in the alignment of actions with a profound purpose. In the realm of purpose-driven leadership, decisions become brushstrokes, contributing to a legacy that transcends mere success.

Maya Angelou's insight further enriches this understanding. "You cannot use up creativity," she asserts.

Purpose-driven leadership, with its focus on aligning decisions with values, becomes a wellspring of creativity. Leaders, fueled by purpose, navigate challenges with innovative solutions deeply rooted in the core values of their organizations.

As leaders embed purpose into their decisions, they embark on a journey where each action contributes to a legacy of creativity, innovation, and lasting impact. Purpose-driven leadership, as a philosophy, becomes a guiding beacon, illuminating a path that leads not only to success but also to a meaningful and impactful journey.

SHAPING A LEGACY BEYOND SUCCESS: SOCIAL IMPACT AS THE INTENTIONAL OUTCOME

Peter Drucker's foresight, "The best way to predict the future is to create it," takes center stage in emphasizing the initiative-taking nature of purpose-driven leadership.

This section explores how purpose-driven leaders go beyond merely responding to the present; they actively shape the future.

Social impact is not treated as a byproduct but as the intentional destination of the leadership journey. Purpose-driven decisions, according to Drucker's perspective, sculpt a legacy that transcends individual achievements. In this progressive and forward-moving leadership, social impact becomes the deliberate outcome of decisions that go beyond the organizational realm.

Mahatma Gandhi's timeless insight, "You must be the change you want to see in the world," becomes a guiding light as leaders craft a legacy through purpose-driven decisions. Purpose-driven leadership inspires leaders to be initiative-taking architects of positive change, leaving an indelible mark on both their organization and the broader societal landscape.

THE ILLUMINATED LEGACY OF PURPOSE-DRIVEN LEADERSHIP: EMBRACING TOMORROW

In conclusion, purpose-driven leadership emerges as a transformative force, illuminating the path forward in the increasingly intricate and ever-evolving landscape of leadership in 2025 and beyond.

At its essence, purpose-driven leadership stands as a beacon of guidance amid the complexities of decision-making.

Rooted in unwavering values, leaders navigate with clarity, ensuring that every choice resonates with the organization's foundational principles. This alignment isn't happenstance; it's a deliberate commitment that steers leaders toward a destination where intentional social impact shapes a legacy beyond mere success—a legacy that resonates with a profound sense of purpose and echoes throughout generations.

As leaders wholeheartedly embrace purpose-driven decision-making, they not only confront today's challenges with resilience but also craft a future that holds greater promise and significance. Through their actions, they become the architects of meaningful change, shaping a landscape characterized by purposeful endeavors and impactful initiatives. Purpose-driven leadership acts as a dynamic force, propelling leaders toward a legacy distinguished by purpose, tangible impact, and enduring success.

Yet, the impact of purpose-driven leadership transcends organizational boundaries. It reverberates through communities, sparking inspiration and igniting change far beyond the confines of the workplace. It fosters a culture of collaboration, empathy, and innovation, paving the way for a future where collective aspirations are realized, and societal progress is achieved.

In essence, purpose-driven leadership isn't merely a strategy—it's a philosophy that infuses every facet of leadership with meaning and significance. It's a commitment to leaving a lasting imprint on the world—a legacy that transcends individual accomplishments and echoes through the annals of history. As leaders embrace purpose-driven principles, they not only shape their organization's trajectory but also contribute to a brighter, more prosperous future for generations to come.

CHAPTER "TO-DO" CHECKLIST

1. **Recognize Purpose as a Guiding Light:**
   Acknowledge purpose-driven leadership as a guiding light that illuminates the path forward.

2. **Embrace Purpose as a Philosophy**:
   Internalize purpose-driven leadership as a luminous philosophy guiding meaningful journeys.

3. **Align Decisions with Core Values**:
   Ensure decisions align with core organizational values guided by purpose.

4. **Infuse Courage into Decision-Making**:
   Embed courage into decisions, drawing inspiration from Winston Churchill.

5. **View Social Impact as Intentional Outcome**:
   Emphasize intentional social impact as a purpose-driven decision's outcome.

6. **Be Initiative-Taking in Shaping the Future**:
   Embrace initiative-taking as architects of positive change, echoing Peter Drucker's insight.

7. **Craft a Legacy beyond Organizational Success**:
   Shape a legacy beyond organizational success, fostering societal impact.

8. **Fuel Creativity through Purpose**:
   Let purpose-driven decisions fuel creativity, echoing Maya Angelou's perspective.

9. **Position Social Impact as Intentional Outcome**:
   Reinforce social impact as an intentional outcome of purpose-driven decisions.

10. **Embrace Initiative-Taking Change**:
    Align with Mahatma Gandhi's insight, embracing initiative-taking for positive change.

FINAL THOUGHTS

Purpose-driven leadership

"Leadership with Purpose: Training Tomorrow's Purpose-Driven Leaders" In the landscape of 2025 and beyond, effective leadership is synonymous with purpose. Training programs must empower leaders to articulate and embody a compelling organizational purpose that goes beyond profit. Leaders trained with a purpose-driven mindset inspire teams, attract top talent, and navigate challenges with resilience. Through purpose-driven leadership training, we shape a future where organizations thrive not only financially but as positive contributors to society.

"The Purpose-Driven Leader: Transformative Training for Tomorrow" Leadership training for 2025 and beyond is a transformative journey into purpose-driven leadership. Leaders are trained not just to manage tasks but to inspire a shared sense of purpose among their teams. Through purpose-driven leadership training, leaders learn to align organizational goals with a higher mission, creating a workplace culture where individuals find fulfillment and collective efforts drive positive impact. The leaders of tomorrow are those who lead with purpose, steering their organizations toward a future defined by meaningful contributions.

These messages underscore the transformative nature of purpose-driven leadership training, emphasizing its ability to inspire, align, and propel organizations toward sustainable success.

CHAPTER QUOTES

1. Maya Angelou:

   You cannot use up creativity.
   https://twitter.com/RoseW1530452/status/1731511
   023662944721

2. Winston Churchill:

   Success is not final, failure is not fatal: It is the courage to continue that count.
   https://www.bsigroup.com/en-GB/blog/Lean-Six-Sigma-Blog/
   12-winston-churchill-quotes-that-encapsulates-a-mindset-
   for-success/#:~:text='Success%20is%20not%20final%2C
   %20failure,to%20get%20what%20you%20want.

3. Peter Drucker:

   The best way to predict the future is to create it.
   https://www.nu.edu/chancellors-page/december-2016/

4. **Henry Ford:**

Failure is not the end but a stepping stone to greater intelligence.
https://www.brainyquote.com/quotes/henry_ford_121339

5. **Mahatma Gandhi:**

You must be the change you want to see in the world.
https://quoteinvestigator.com/2017/10/23/be-change/

6. **Jean de La Bruyère:**
   • "The most profound transformations often emerge from the soil of difficulties, as resilience turns challenges into steppingstones."
   https://www.goodreads.com/author/quotes/778012.Jean_de_La_Bruy_re
   • "Out of difficulties grow miracles."
   https://www.goodreads.com/author/quotes/778012.Jean_de_La_Bruy_re
   • "The most profound transformations often emerge from the soil of difficulties, as resilience turns challenges into stepping stones."
   https://www.goodreads.com/author/quotes/778012.Jean_de_La_Bruy_re

7. **Jodi Picoult:**

The human capacity for burden is like bamboo—far more flexible than you'd ever believe at first glance.
https://www.goodreads.com/quotes/166675-the-human-capacity-for-burden-is-like-bamboo--far-more

8. **Charles R. Swindoll:**

Life is 10% what happens to us and 90% how we react to it.
https://www.goodreads.com/author/quotes/5139.Charles_R_Swindoll

Purpose-driven leadership illuminates the path forward, where values become the compass, and social impact is the destination. In each decision, leaders sculpt a legacy that echoes not only success but a profound sense of purpose, leaving an indelible mark on both the organization and the world.

—Douglas Pflug

Chapter 4

Authenticity in Leadership

VALUING GENUINE AND TRANSPARENT LEADERSHIP STYLES THAT RESONATE WITH INDIVIDUALS ON A PERSONAL LEVEL

Photo Credit: Nick Fewings https://unsplash.com/

Authenticity in leadership is the beacon that lights the way for meaningful connections. When leaders embrace their genuine selves with transparency and sincerity, they forge a profound bond that transcends titles. In the symphony of leadership, authenticity is the melody that resonates in the hearts of those who follow, creating a harmonious and impactful journey together.

—Douglas Pflug

DOI: 10.1201/9781003518099-6

MY THOUGHTS AND COMMENTARY

> Resilience cultivation is the art of growing stronger in the face of storms, a testament to the human spirit's ability to bloom amidst challenges. Plant the seeds of a positive mindset, water them with perseverance, and watch as the garden of resilience flourishes, turning setbacks into steppingstones on the path to triumph.

Throughout my career, I have found myself entangled in the intricate dynamics of organizational silos that operate discreetly behind the scenes, whether by choice or circumstance. Unfortunately, in many organizations, the team often influences the trajectory of advancement, promotions, or enhanced opportunities you align with and the strategies you employ.

In maneuvering through this intricate landscape, my constant endeavor has been to align myself with a team that transcends the conventional notions of being just a team member. This effort was driven not by a desire to avoid the strategic maneuvers often associated with organizational dynamics but by a sincere commitment to the shared empathy and constructive collaboration that characterize a cohesive team.

While I intended to distance myself from the notion of "playing the game," it became evident that I was still part of a team—not merely for the sake of association but due to a genuine dedication to the collective spirit and collaborative energy that a team embodies. My participation in the organizational game has not been that of a passive onlooker but rather that of an empathetic contributor fully engaged in the collaborative process.

Regardless of the team dynamics or the particular angle I found myself approaching the concept of teamwork, I have remained steadfast in my commitment to authenticity, realness, and being true to myself. In an environment that may at times prioritize conformity or strategic alliances, staying genuine has been my anchor.

For me, my goal was to be authentic in all personal and professional settings, involving embracing one's unique qualities, perspectives, and values. It means navigating the organizational landscape with a sense of integrity that transcends the prevailing game-playing culture. Instead of succumbing to the pressures of conformity, I have consistently chosen to bring my true self to the table.

Authenticity to me is not about being a passive observer or a contrarian. It is about aligning personal values with professional actions, staying true to one's beliefs, and expressing genuine intentions even when faced with challenges.

This commitment to authenticity has not only shaped my professional identity but has also contributed to fostering a culture of sincerity within the teams I have been a part of.

In essence, the journey has been about finding a delicate balance between active participation in the organizational game and remaining true to my core values. It is a continuous process of self-discovery and self-expression, where authenticity becomes not just a personal choice but a beacon that guides interactions, decisions, and relationships in the ever-evolving landscape of the professional world.

Always remember and be guided by doing the right thing because it is the right thing to do and in default,

> Right is right even if no one is doing it; wrong is wrong even if everyone is doing it.
>
> —Saint Augustine

WHAT DO HISTORY AND GENERAL RESEARCH ILLUSTRATE TO US?

Introduction: The imperative of resilience in leadership

In the ever-evolving tapestry of leadership, resilience emerges as a foundational element, a dynamic process that sets apart leaders capable of thriving amid the storms of uncertainty. Resilience is not a static quality but an evolving art, a testament to the indomitable spirit of the human experience. Leaders, as stewards of this art, navigate the journey of turning setbacks into steppingstones, fostering an environment where the human spirit triumphs over adversity.

In progressive thinking and forward-moving leadership, resilience is not merely a trait; it is an art—a dynamic process that leaders can master, ensuring they guide their teams through challenges with unwavering strength.

Yes, there is a difference between personal resilience and leadership resilience. While both concepts share some similarities, they operate in distinct contexts and have different emphases.

WHAT IS THE DIFFERENCE BETWEEN PERSONAL AND LEADERSHIP RESILIENCY?

Personal resilience is about an individual's ability to navigate challenges in their personal life, focusing on emotional and psychological well-being. Leadership resilience, on the other hand, expands this concept to the professional realm, emphasizing how leaders guide organizations through difficulties, make strategic decisions, and maintain stability in the face of adversity.

While personal and leadership resilience is interconnected, leadership resilience has a broader scope and emphasizes the organizational impact of resilience in a leadership role.

PERSONAL RESILIENCE

- Focus on Individuals: Personal resilience primarily revolves around an individual's ability to bounce back from challenges, setbacks, and adversity in their personal life. It is a characteristic that helps individuals maintain mental well-being and cope with stressors, both in and outside the workplace.
- Psychological Well-Being: Personal resilience often involves aspects of emotional and psychological well-being. Individuals with high personal resilience can adapt to change, manage stress, and maintain a positive outlook in their personal lives.
- Coping Mechanisms: Developing personal resilience may involve the cultivation of coping mechanisms, self-awareness, and a mindset that views challenges as opportunities for growth.

LEADERSHIP RESILIENCE

- Applied in a Leadership Context: Leadership resilience, on the other hand, is focused on how leaders navigate challenges and uncertainties within the organizational and professional context. It extends beyond an individual's personal life and into their role as a leader.
- Organizational Impact: Leadership resilience considers how leaders respond to crises, lead teams through change, and make decisions under pressure. It involves the ability to steer an organization through challenges, inspire confidence in the team, and maintain a strategic focus.
- Strategic Vision and Decision-Making: Leaders with resilience at the leadership level often have a strategic vision, can make decisions that benefit the organization in the long term and can maintain composure during times of crisis.

THE ART OF RESILIENCE CULTIVATION: NURTURING INNER STRENGTH

Jodi Picoult's eloquent analogy paints a vivid picture of resilience—the inherent flexibility of the human spirit, capable of bending without breaking. Cultivating resilience becomes an art that requires a conscious commitment to strengthening in the face of uncertainty.

> The human capacity for burden is like bamboo—far more flexible than you'd ever believe at first glance.
>
> —Jodi Picoult

In this progressive leadership paradigm, the art of resilience is symbolized by the ever-flexible bamboo, thriving amid the storms of challenges. Leaders are tasked with embracing challenges as opportunities for growth, fostering a culture where setbacks are seen as temporary obstacles on the path to triumph.

> Life is not merely about what happens to us but how we choose to react.
> —Charles R. Swindoll

PLANTING THE SEEDS OF A POSITIVE MINDSET: FOSTERING OPTIMISM AMID CHALLENGES

Charles R. Swindoll's poignant quote encapsulates the transformative power of mindset in resilience cultivation. Leaders are urged to cultivate an optimistic outlook, viewing setbacks as temporary and opportunities for learning and growth.

> Life is 10% what happens to us and 90% how we react to it.
> —Charles R. Swindoll

Within the fertile soil of a positive mindset, the seeds of resilience germinate, growing into a garden of opportunities amid life's challenges. Cultivating a positive mindset becomes more than a personal endeavor; it becomes a leadership strategy with a ripple effect on the entire team.

> The most profound transformations often emerge from the soil of difficulties, as resilience turns challenges into stepping stones.
> —Jean de La Bruyère

WATERING WITH PERSEVERANCE: NURTURING THE SEEDS OF RESILIENCE

Albert Einstein's wisdom places a spotlight on the critical role of perseverance in resilience cultivation. Watering the seeds of resilience involves staying committed to the process of growth, even when faced with challenges and setbacks.

> It's not that I'm so smart, it's just that I stay with problems longer.
> —Albert Einstein

In progressive leadership thinking, perseverance becomes the constant rainfall that nurtures the seeds of resilience, ensuring they grow into steadfast plants capable of weathering any storm. Leaders take on the role of caretakers, ensuring that the garden of resilience is consistently nurtured.

> Failure is simply the opportunity to begin again, this time more intelligently.
>
> —Henry Ford

THE GARDEN OF RESILIENCE FLOURISHES: TRIUMPH AMID CHALLENGES

Jean de La Bruyère's profound quote encapsulates the transformative potential of resilience—the ability to turn difficulties into opportunities for growth and miracles. In the garden of resilience, setbacks become stepping stones on the path to triumph.

> Out of difficulties grow miracles.
>
> —Jean de La Bruyère

This emphasizes that resilience is not a passive state but an active process that involves learning, adapting, and thriving in the face of uncertainty. Leaders are encouraged to create an environment where resilience is not just a personal attribute but a shared value that permeates the organizational culture.

> Failure is not the end but a stepping stone to greater intelligence.
>
> —Henry Ford

TURNING SETBACKS INTO STEPPINGSTONES: THE RECIPE OF RESILIENCE

Henry Ford's timeless quote underscores the transformative nature of setbacks—they are not the end but an opportunity to begin again with greater insight and intelligence. This explores the art of turning setbacks into stepping stones, emphasizing the role of resilience in reframing failures as valuable learning experiences.

> Failure is simply the opportunity to begin again, this time more intelligently.
>
> —Henry Ford

In the journey of leadership, setbacks become the raw materials that resilient leaders masterfully craft into stepping stones, paving the way to greater intelligence and success. Leaders become alchemists, turning the raw materials of setbacks into the gold of wisdom and experience. This guides leaders in navigating the alchemy of resilience, where failures are not feared but embraced as opportunities for growth.

CONCLUSION: A GARDEN OF TRIUMPH IN THE LEADERSHIP LANDSCAPE

In conclusion, the cultivation of resilience is not just a survival strategy; it is an art form that transforms the leadership landscape. As leaders plant the seeds of a positive mindset, water them with perseverance, and see the garden of resilience flourishing, they redefine triumph in the face of adversity.

This urges leaders to embrace resilience not as a reactive measure but as an initiative-taking approach to growth and success. In the garden of triumph, setbacks are not roadblocks but pathways to greater intelligence, innovation, and lasting success. Leaders are encouraged to be both gardeners and architects, cultivating resilience within themselves and fostering a culture where the entire organizational landscape is characterized by artful triumph over challenges.

CHAPTER "TO-DO" CHECKLIST

1. **Establish Resilience as a Cornerstone:**
   Portray resilience as essential for leaders to thrive amid challenges.

2. **Emphasize Resilience as an Evolving Art:**
   Define resilience as dynamic, urging leaders to navigate storms and emerge stronger.

3. **Metaphorically Explore Resilience:**
   Utilize Jodi Picoult's bamboo analogy to showcase resilience, highlighting the human spirit's ability to bend without breaking.

4. **Encourage Recognition of Flexibility:**
   Urge leaders to acknowledge flexibility within themselves and their teams, seeing challenges as growth opportunities.

5. **Highlight Positive Mindset as a Catalyst:**
   Emphasize Charles R. Swindoll's quote on mindset's transformative power for resilience.

6. **Cultivate a Positive Mindset:**
   Explore strategies like reframing challenges and embracing gratitude to foster resilience.

7. **Stress the Importance of Perseverance:**
   Highlight Albert Einstein's insight on perseverance as crucial for resilience.

8. **Model Perseverance for Teams:**
   Encourage leaders to exemplify perseverance, showing its importance in overcoming difficulties.

9. **Showcase Triumph Amid Challenges:**
   Illustrate resilience in action as leaders and teams achieve success amid adversity.

10. **Reframe Setbacks as Stepping Stones:**
    Guide leaders in turning setbacks into opportunities for growth and increased resilience.

FINAL THOUGHTS

Authenticity in Leadership:

"Authentic Leadership Mastery: Training Tomorrow's Genuine Leaders"
In the dynamic landscape of 2025 and beyond, authenticity is the currency of effective leadership. Training programs must immerse leaders in the art of authentic leadership, emphasizing self-awareness and genuine connection. Leaders trained in authenticity inspire trust, foster open communication, and create an organizational culture where individuals feel empowered to bring their true selves to work. Authentic leadership training is the cornerstone of building resilient and engaged teams for the future.

"Leading from Within: Authenticity at the Core of Tomorrow's Leaders"
Leadership training for 2025 and beyond is a journey into leading from within. Authenticity is not just a leadership trait; it's a transformative force that shapes organizational culture. Through authentic leadership training, leaders learn to embrace their unique strengths, vulnerabilities, and values. This training empowers leaders to build genuine connections, navigate challenges with integrity, and create workplaces where authenticity is not just encouraged but celebrated.

These messages highlight the pivotal role of authenticity in leadership training, emphasizing its power to build trust, foster open communication, and create resilient organizational cultures.

CHAPTER QUOTES

1. Jean de La Bruyère

   Out of difficulties grow miracles.

   https://www.brainyquote.com/quotes/jean_de_la_
   bruyere_380158

2. Albert Einstein

   It's not that I'm so smart, it's just that I stay with problems longer.

   https://www.brainyquote.com/quotes/albert_
   einstein_106192

3. Henry Ford

   Failure is simply the opportunity to begin again, this time more intelligently.

   https://www.brainyquote.com/quotes/henry_
   ford_121339

4. Jodi Picoult

   The human capacity for burden is like bamboo—far more flexible than you'd ever believe at first glance.

   https://www.goodreads.com/quotes/166675-the-human-
   capacity-for-burden-is-like-bamboo--far-more

5. Charles R. Swindoll

   Life is 10% what happens to us and 90% how we react to it.

   https://www.brainyquote.com/quotes/charles_r_
   swindoll_388332

Authenticity in leadership is the beacon that lights the way for meaningful connections. When leaders embrace their genuine selves with transparency and sincerity, they forge a profound bond that transcends titles. In the symphony of leadership, authenticity is the melody that resonates in the hearts of those who follow, creating a harmonious and impactful journey together.

—Douglas Pflug

Part 2

Time to Take This to a New Level

Photo credit: Casey Hirner https://unsplash.com

As we stand on the brink of 2025 and beyond, it's time to elevate our game with personal leadership. Let's collectively take it to the next level, not just for ourselves, but to inspire and empower everyone on this transformative journey of growth and success.

—Douglas Pflug

DOI: 10.1201/9781003518099-7

Chapter 5

Remote Leadership Skills

DEVELOPING EFFECTIVE LEADERSHIP ABILITIES IN VIRTUAL AND REMOTE WORK ENVIRONMENTS

Photo Credit: Carolyn Christine https://unsplash.com/

Remote leadership skills thrive in the digital landscape, where influence transcends distance. Cultivate the art of guiding teams through screens, fostering connection, and inspiring collaboration—a testament to the adaptability and strength of leadership in the virtual realm.

—Douglas Pflug

DOI: 10.1201/9781003518099-8

MY THOUGHTS AND COMMENTARY

Remote leadership skills thrive in the digital landscape, where influence transcends distance. Cultivate the art of guiding teams through screens, fostering connection, and inspiring collaboration—a testament to the adaptability and strength of leadership in the virtual realm.

Upon retiring from policing and transitioning to the leadership unit of the Ontario Police College, my role primarily involved on-site teaching, constituting around 90% of my responsibilities. Residing in Guelph, I had a 70-minute commute, which I found beneficial as it afforded me the necessary time to prepare and establish the right mindset for my work. Conversely, the journey home provided ample time for decompression, allowing me to leave work-related matters behind by the time I reached home. I emphasize to all my supervisors the importance of preparing for work and equally preparing for home.

The commute, whether heading to or from work, served as a valuable transition. It allowed "Doug" to be present at home and "Mr. Pflug" to be fully engaged at work, ensuring a clear separation of personal and professional responsibilities.

After a year of working, I approached a manager to explore the possibility of transitioning from a traditional 5x8 hour schedule to either a compressed 4x10 hour or 3x12 hour shift schedule, particularly when I was not engaged in teaching but rather managing administrative office duties. I aimed to enhance work-life balance by spending an additional day(s) at home each week and to save on commuting costs.

Unfortunately, my request was denied, with the manager expressing a belief that such an alternative work arrangement would never be allowed.

This decision reflected the entrenched mindset of "We've never done it that way," a mentality often encountered in policing. In policing we also see the double-edged sword of "people hate when things stay the same" and "people hate when things change."

I have consistently felt discomfort in environments where this sentiment prevails, as it conveys resistance to change while simultaneously expressing dissatisfaction with the status quo. Quite simply, when change arises, I look at it as an opportunity to learn and grow.

In March 2020, when the global impact of COVID-19 became evident, the familiar landscape of our world underwent a profound transformation. Established thought processes were cast aside, and we were mandated to shift to exclusive remote work.

Additionally, a sizable portion of our courses was suspended due to the evident concerns surrounding the spread of the disease.

Entering 2021, our courses were gradually reinstated on a case-by-case basis, while the option to work remotely from home remained in effect. This arrangement proved exceptionally beneficial, as I discovered that I could accomplish a higher workload from home without continuous interruptions related to work issues or impromptu interactions.

Keeping track of my actual work hours and tasks completed using an Excel sheet, I observed that on any given day, I was logging more hours than I typically would at my physical workplace, and without the 70-minute commute on both ends. This transition to remote work brought about two notable improvements—I became a more effective employee and found an enhanced balance in managing responsibilities at home.

The morale of my colleagues and myself dropped dramatically.

In July 2023, three years into remote work, we received a directive to return to on-site attendance three days a week. When we questioned the rationale behind this decision, the response was a unilateral "We've always done it that way," and thus, we were reverting to the previous arrangement.

Despite various pleas presented by individuals outlining their specific cases, all requests were denied, and we were compelled to resume on-site work three days a week.

The administration's insistence on a 12–14 week per year travel requirement, coupled with the demand for in-office presence when remote work was feasible, significantly impacted our families and work-life balance.

The old-school leadership mentality prevailing in our organization, rooted in the 1980s, failed to adapt to modern expectations of work-life balance, leading to frustration among employees.

This leadership approach is evident in the unequal treatment of employees, as some have informal arrangements allowing minimal office attendance, while others, despite seeking similar considerations, face denials. The expectation for a three-day office presence, despite no on-site courses and a 2.5-hour commute, is causing personal and financial strain, with associated costs for lodging and dining out impacting dietary habits.

The reluctance to embrace remote work or a flexible hybrid model is concerning, especially given the potential benefits recognized during and post-COVID-19. Flexibility, cost savings, increased productivity, and reduced commute stress are advantages, but challenges such as isolation, communication issues, blurred work-life boundaries, technological hurdles, and the potential for overworking need consideration.

As we enter 2024, leadership must adapt to the changing work landscape. Outdated practices may result in a shortage of employees, as individuals seek alternatives to enhance overall well-being and productivity. A multi-generational workforce is calling for remote work options or a flexible hybrid model, emphasizing the importance of open-minded, progressive leadership.

In summary, while working from home offers significant benefits, a thoughtful consideration of individual and organizational needs is essential. Hybrid models that balance remote and in-office work may be the key to addressing the complexities of the post-COVID-19 work environment.

WHAT DO HISTORY AND GENERAL RESEARCH ILLUSTRATE TO US?

Introduction: The symphony of remote leadership skills in 2025 and beyond

Stepping into the digital era of 2025 and beyond, the dynamics of leadership undergo a profound transformation shaped by the digital landscape. In this context, the unique skills required for remote leadership take center stage, transcending traditional boundaries of physical proximity. Leaders are challenged to cultivate a set of skills that not only navigate the complexities of the digital realm but also foster genuine connection and collaboration.

The adaptability and strength of leadership are put to the test in this virtual era, where the harmonious melody of remote leadership skills resonates across digital spaces, proving the enduring influence of leadership that transcends physical distance.

> The greatest leader is not necessarily the one who does the greatest things. He is the one that gets the people to do the greatest things.
> —Ronald Reagan

THE ART OF GUIDING TEAMS THROUGH THE VIRTUAL REALM

Charles Darwin's evolutionary perspective becomes a guiding principle in understanding the art of guiding teams through screens. This underscores the adaptive and responsive nature of leadership in navigating the challenges of the digital landscape. In this context, remote leadership is not merely about overcoming challenges but embracing an evolutionary shift that demands a nuanced approach to guiding and leading teams.

As leaders adapt their skills to guide teams through screens, the words of Steve Jobs become a beacon, positioning innovation as the key distinguishing factor for leaders in the realm of remote leadership. Remote leadership is not just about adapting to change; it is about innovating in the way teams collaborate, communicate, and achieve shared goals.

Innovation distinguishes between a leader and a follower.

—Steve Jobs

FOSTERING CONNECTION: BUILDING DIGITAL BRIDGES ACROSS DISTANCES

Phil Jackson's insight becomes the focal point in exploring the importance of fostering connection in remote leadership. This emphasizes the collective strength derived from individual contributions, even in a virtual setting.

Leaders are encouraged to foster a sense of connection that goes beyond the physical boundaries of an office, creating a digital environment where each team member feels valued and integral to the team's success.

As leaders build digital bridges across distances, the words of Richard Branson become a guiding principle, positioning communication as a pivotal skill for leaders in remote settings. Fostering connection in remote leadership involves effective communication strategies that bridge the gap between physical distances and ensure a cohesive and motivated team.

The strength of the team is each member. The strength of each member is the team.

—Phil Jackson

INSPIRING COLLABORATION: CULTIVATING A VIRTUAL CULTURE OF COOPERATION

Helen Keller's timeless wisdom becomes a cornerstone in understanding the essence of inspiring collaboration in the digital era. This explores how leaders can cultivate a virtual culture of cooperation that transcends the limitations of physical separation.

Leaders are encouraged to inspire collaboration by leveraging digital tools, fostering a sense of shared purpose, and creating a collaborative environment that encourages innovation and shared success.

As leaders inspire collaboration in remote teams, the words of Simon Sinek become a guiding light, emphasizing the tangible outcomes and effectiveness of a culture of collaboration. Inspiring collaboration in the digital landscape is not just about camaraderie; it is about achieving tangible outcomes that propel the team toward success.

We live by each other and for each other. Alone we can do so little; together we can do so much.

—Helen Keller

CONCLUSION: THE RESILIENCE AND STRENGTH OF REMOTE LEADERSHIP SKILLS

In conclusion, the landscape of leadership in 2025 and beyond is intricately tied to the digital realm. Remote leadership skills are not just adaptations to a changing environment; they are a harmonious melody in the symphony of leadership. The art of guiding teams through screens, fostering connection, and inspiring collaboration is a testament to the adaptability and strength of leadership in the virtual era.

As leaders embrace and cultivate these skills, they not only navigate the complexities of the digital landscape but also thrive, proving that the essence of leadership transcends physical distances and manifests in the enduring influence of guiding and inspiring teams in the virtual realm.

The conclusion reinforces the idea that remote leadership skills are not mere adaptations but a harmonious melody in the symphony of leadership, highlighting their enduring influence. It emphasizes the adaptability and strength needed in navigating the digital landscape and positions leadership as a force that transcends physical distances, guiding and inspiring teams in the virtual realm with enduring influence.

> Leadership is not about being in charge. It is about taking care of those in your charge.
>
> —Simon Sinek

CHAPTER "TO-DO" CHECKLIST

1. **Acknowledge Digital Influence:**
   Recognize the ongoing impact of the digital landscape on leadership.

2. **Prioritize Remote Leadership Skills:**
   Understand remote leadership skills as vital in modern leadership.

3. **Embrace Adaptability:**
   Embrace adaptability in guiding teams digitally, echoing Charles Darwin's wisdom.

4. **Innovate Remote Leadership:**
   Internalize the need for innovative approaches in remote leadership, reshaping collaboration methods.

5. **Foster Connection across Digital Spaces:**
   Prioritize fostering connections beyond physical boundaries in remote leadership.

6. **Highlight Collective Strength:**
   Emphasize the strength derived from individual team members in remote collaboration.

7. **Communicate Effectively:**
   Acknowledge the pivotal role of effective communication in virtual team cohesion.

8. **Inspire Collaboration in Virtual Culture:**
   Cultivate a culture of virtual collaboration, echoing Helen Keller's perspective on teamwork.

9. **Utilize Digital Tools for Collaboration:**
   Leverage digital tools to inspire collaboration and innovation within remote teams.

10. **Value Tangible Outcomes:**
    Recognize the importance of achieving tangible outcomes in fostering a collaborative culture.

FINAL THOUGHTS

Remote Leadership Skills:

"Remote Leadership Mastery: Training Leaders for the Digital Frontier"
In the evolving landscape of 2025 and beyond, leadership training is a journey into remote leadership mastery. Leaders are trained not only to adapt but to excel in leading virtual teams. Through remote leadership training, leaders gain essential skills in virtual communication, team engagement, and technology utilization. Training programs prepare leaders to navigate the challenges of remote work, fostering collaboration, and ensuring that distance does not hinder productivity or team cohesion.

"Leading Beyond Boundaries: Remote Leadership Skills for Tomorrow's Leaders"

Leadership training in 2025 is about leading beyond physical boundaries. Remote leadership skills become a strategic imperative, and training programs focus on equipping leaders with the tools to thrive in a virtual environment. Leaders learn to leverage technology for effective communication, build a remote-friendly culture, and lead with empathy, ensuring that teams not only adapt but excel in a distributed work setting.

These messages underscore the importance of remote leadership skills in the evolving landscape, emphasizing the need for leaders to be proficient in managing and inspiring teams in virtual environments.

CHAPTER QUOTES

1. Ronald Reagan

> The greatest leader is not necessarily the one who does the greatest things. He is the one that gets the people to do the greatest things.
> https://www.phoneburner.com/blog/8-inspiring-leadership-quotes-2

2. Phil Jackson

> The strength of the team is each member. The strength of each member is the team.
> https://www.brainyquote.com/quotes/phil_jackson_210184

3. Steve Jobs

> Innovation distinguishes between a leader and a follower.
> https://www.forbes.com/sites/bwoo/2013/02/14/innovation-distinguishes-between-a-leader-and-a-follower/?sh=45ba7a4f2844

4. Helen Keller

> Alone, we can do so little; together, we can do so much.
> https://www.brainyquote.com/quotes/helen_keller_382259

5. Simon Sinek

> Leadership is not about being in charge. It is about taking care of those in your charge.
> https://sohailzindani.medium.com/leadership-is-not-about-being-in-charge-f2af0827bf83

Remote leadership skills thrive in the digital landscape, where influence transcends distance. Cultivate the art of guiding teams through screens, fostering connection, and inspiring collaboration—a testament to the adaptability and strength of leadership in the virtual realm.

—Douglas Pflug

Chapter 6

Art of Adaptive Learning

EMBRACING A CONTINUOUS LEARNING MINDSET TO ADAPT TO EVOLVING CHALLENGES AND OPPORTUNITIES

Photo Credit: Andrew Neal https://unsplash.com/

Adaptive learning is the compass of progress, navigating the ever-shifting landscape of challenges and opportunities. Embrace the rhythm of continuous learning, for in its cadence lies the melody of resilience, innovation, and the perpetual dance with the evolving tapestry of knowledge.

—Douglas Pflug

DOI: 10.1201/9781003518099-9

MY THOUGHTS AND COMMENTARY

Adaptive learning is the compass of progress, navigating the ever-shifting landscape of challenges and opportunities. Embrace the rhythm of continuous learning, for in its cadence lies the melody of resilience, innovation, and the perpetual dance with the evolving tapestry of knowledge.

As I navigate the later stages of my 35-year career in law enforcement, concluding my 28 years of service with the Guelph Police Service as a Sergeant and spending the last 7 years as a leadership instructor at the Ontario Police College, I find myself growing more mindful, nostalgic, and excited about the possibilities that lie ahead in my future.

Since 2015, I have acknowledged the inevitability of our expiration dates. Embracing this reality, I actively sought opportunities to gain a profound understanding of my past, present, and future aspirations.

Witnessing numerous leaders, politicians, and sports stars persist beyond their expiration dates, departing not at the peak but rather in a state of embarrassment, fatigue, and physical or emotional injury, I made a personal vow that my journey would not follow that path. Simultaneously, I have held onto the ethos of "I'll rest when I'm dead."

In that spirit, I would like to share three personal and professional template goals that I believe will better enhance my life, and I hope they will yours as well:

SELF-REFLECTION AND SELF-AWARENESS

I dedicate time to regular self-reflection to understand my own emotions, triggers, and reactions. This introspective practice enhances my self-awareness, a fundamental aspect of emotional intelligence. Actively journaling and participating in mindfulness exercises, I deepen my understanding of my emotional responses in various situations.

EMPATHY IN ACTION

I actively practice empathy in my daily interactions, with a simple goal of making at least one stranger smile per day. I reflect on each smile I help create every day during my nightly prayers, starting and ending my day with positive thoughts.

I always take a moment to reflect by putting myself in others' shoes, striving to understand their perspectives and emotions. I challenge myself to listen actively, validate others' feelings, and respond with empathy. I genuinely seek to understand not just the words spoken but the emotions behind them. This empathetic approach strengthens my values and corresponding connection with others, contributing to a more harmonious environment.

CONTINUOUS LEARNING AND DEVELOPMENT

Emotional intelligence is a skill that I consistently strive to refine and expand upon in everyone's life. Engaging in continuous learning opportunities to further develop my emotional intelligence, I have pursued academic pursuits at Cornell University, recently at McMaster University, and delved into literature on emotional intelligence. Attending workshops or training sessions and seeking feedback from others on my people skills are additional steps I take.

The more I invest in honing my emotional intelligence, the more adept I become at navigating the complexities of human connections and assisting others in improving their emotional intelligence. This investment deeply improved my ability to coach, counsel, mentor, and instruct others.

Note: Improving emotional intelligence is an ongoing process that involves consistent self-awareness and a commitment to understanding and connecting with others on a deeper emotional level.

I am committed to the task; are you?

WHAT DO HISTORY AND GENERAL RESEARCH ILLUSTRATE TO US?

Introduction: The symphony of adaptive learning

As we step into the dynamic era of leadership in 2025 and beyond, the ability to adapt becomes paramount.

This exploration delves into the transformative power of adaptive learning—a compass that not only guides leaders through challenges and opportunities but also shapes the melody of resilience and innovation. The journey of leadership evolves into a perpetual dance, with the rhythm of continuous learning at its core.

In the realm of progressive thinking and forward-moving leadership, adaptive learning transcends being a mere skill; it is a mindset—a compass that propels leaders forward in the ever-evolving landscape, navigating the complexities with agility and foresight.

The introduction sets the stage for this chapter, positioning adaptive learning as more than a skill—it is a mindset. Emphasizing the dynamic nature of leadership in an ever-evolving landscape, it introduces the concept of a symphony where adaptive learning is the guiding force orchestrating a harmonious blend of resilience and innovation.

THE ESSENCE OF ADAPTIVE LEARNING: A COMPASS FOR PROGRESS

> Learning and innovation go hand in hand. The arrogance of success is to think that what you did yesterday will be sufficient for tomorrow.
> —William Pollard

William Pollard's profound perspective serves as the cornerstone of this section, emphasizing the inseparable link between learning and innovation.

This section further explores adaptive learning as a compass for progress, steering leaders away from the arrogance of stagnation. It encourages leaders to cultivate a culture that embraces the continual pursuit of knowledge, recognizing that relying on yesterday's solutions may not suffice for tomorrow's challenges.

In the realm of progressive thinking and forward-moving leadership, William Pollard's words resonate deeply adaptive learning is not merely a response to challenges; it is an initiative-taking approach to navigating the ever-shifting landscape.

As leaders embrace adaptive learning, John C. Maxwell's insight becomes a guiding principle—the greatest mistake is living in constant fear of making one. Within the leadership landscape, adaptive learning liberates leaders from the fear of mistakes, fostering a culture where experimentation and growth are not just accepted but celebrated.

John C. Maxwell's quote reinforces the idea that adaptive learning liberates leaders from the fear of mistakes, fostering a culture that not only values experimentation but views mistakes as opportunities for growth and improvement.

CONTINUOUS LEARNING AS A MELODY: A CADENCE OF RESILIENCE

> It is not the strongest of the species that survive, nor the most intelligent, but the one most responsive to change.
> —Charles Darwin

Charles Darwin's timeless wisdom takes center stage in this section, highlighting the profound connection between adaptability and survival. The exploration of continuous learning, akin to a melodic cadence, fortifies leaders and their teams with resilience.

Leaders are encouraged to perceive challenges not as insurmountable obstacles but as opportunities for growth. Understanding that the ability to respond to change is the true measure of strength becomes paramount.

In the realm of progressive thinking and forward-moving leadership, Charles Darwin's words echo—the melody of continuous learning is the key to resilience, enabling leaders to navigate challenges with agility and fortitude.

As leaders embrace the cadence of continuous learning, Peter Drucker's wisdom becomes a guiding light—the best way to predict the future is to create it. Adaptive learning empowers leaders to actively shape their future, positioning themselves as architects of innovation and progress.

Peter Drucker's insight underscores the initiative-taking nature of adaptive learning, empowering leaders not just to predict but to actively shape their future through continuous innovation and progress.

INNOVATION UNLEASHED: THE PERPETUAL DANCE WITH KNOWLEDGE

> The illiterate of the 21st century will not be those who cannot read and write, but those who cannot learn, unlearn, and relearn.
> —Alvin Toffler

Alvin Toffler's foresight becomes the focal point of this section, emphasizing the importance of unlearning and relearning in the landscape of leadership. This exploration delves into how adaptive learning fuels the perpetual dance with knowledge, liberating leaders from the shackles of outdated paradigms.

Leaders are encouraged to foster an environment that not only accepts change but embraces it, recognizing that innovation thrives when knowledge is dynamic and evolving.

In progressive thinking and forward-moving leadership, Alvin Toffler's words reverberate—the perpetual dance with knowledge requires leaders to be agile learners, unlearning and relearning as the tempo of progress accelerates.

As leaders engage in the perpetual dance with knowledge, Mahatma Gandhi's insight becomes a guiding principle—live as if you were to die tomorrow and learn as if you were to live forever. Adaptive learning propels leaders to live in the moment while preparing for a future characterized by continuous growth and evolution.

Mahatma Gandhi's wisdom highlights the timelessness of learning, positioning adaptive learning as a lifelong journey that combines living in the present with preparing for a future characterized by continuous growth and evolution.

CONCLUSION: HARMONIZING LEADERSHIP WITH ADAPTIVE LEARNING

In conclusion, adaptive learning emerges as the compass of progress, guiding leaders through the ever-shifting landscape of challenges and opportunities. The melody of resilience and innovation intricately weaves into the cadence of continuous learning—a rhythm that defines the symphony of leadership in 2025 and beyond.

As leaders embrace the perpetual dance with the evolving tapestry of knowledge, they not only navigate change but become architects of a future where adaptability is the hallmark of success. In this symphony, adaptive learning is not just a skill; it is the harmonizing force that propels leaders and their organizations toward a crescendo of growth and triumph.

This reinforces the interconnectedness of adaptive learning, resilience, and innovation in the symphony of leadership. It positions adaptive learning as the harmonizing force that propels leaders toward a future marked by continuous growth and triumph, creating a powerful and optimistic note to conclude the chapter.

Author's suggested points to accomplish this goal

1. **Foster a Culture of Lifelong Learning:**
   Encourage a culture where continuous learning is embraced at all levels of the organization, fostering adaptability and innovation.

2. **Encourage Experimentation and Risk-Taking:**
   Promote a culture where experimentation and risk-taking are valued, allowing for the exploration of new ideas and approaches.

3. **Invest in Learning Technologies:**
   Allocate resources to invest in learning technologies that facilitate adaptive learning and skill development across remote and diverse teams.

4. **Promote Cross-Functional Collaboration:**
   Encourage collaboration across departments and disciplines, fostering diverse perspectives and collective problem-solving.

5. **Recognize and Reward Adaptability:**
   Implement systems to recognize and reward adaptability and innovative thinking, reinforcing their importance within the organization's culture.

6. **Provide Mentorship and Coaching:**
   Offer mentorship and coaching programs to support employees in their ongoing learning and development journey.

7. **Foster a Growth Mindset:**
Cultivate a growth mindset within the organization, encouraging employees to see challenges as opportunities for learning and growth.

8. **Stay Agile and Flexible:**
Maintain agility and flexibility in processes and structures, allowing the organization to adapt quickly to changing circumstances and opportunities.

9. **Encourage Knowledge Sharing:**
Facilitate platforms and initiatives for knowledge sharing and peer learning, harnessing the collective intelligence of the organization.

10. **Lead by Example:**
Leaders should embody a commitment to adaptive learning and continuous improvement, serving as role models for their teams and inspiring others to embrace lifelong learning.

CHAPTER "TO-DO" CHECKLIST

1. **Acknowledge Adaptive Learning as a Mindset:**
Recognize adaptive learning as a mindset crucial for navigating evolving leadership landscapes.

2. **Align Decisions with Core Values:**
Foster a culture aligning decisions with core values, driven by an adaptive learning approach.

3. **Embrace Mistakes as Opportunities:**
Liberally view mistakes as learning opportunities, echoing John C. Maxwell's perspective.

4. **View Continuous Learning as Resilience:**
Recognize continuous learning as a resilience-building melody for leaders.

5. **Position Continuous Learning as a Resilience Tool:**
Emphasize continuous learning's role in developing leaders' resilience and adaptability.

6. **Empower Leaders to Shape the Future:**
Echo Peter Drucker's wisdom, showcasing how adaptive learning empowers leaders to architect innovation and progress.

7. **Highlight Unlearning and Relearning:**
   Underscore the importance of unlearning and relearning, inspired by Alvin Toffler's foresight.

8. **Encourage Agility in Learning:**
   Promote agility in learning, emphasizing flexibility and adaptability in the process.

9. **Stress the Timelessness of Learning:**
   Reinforce Mahatma Gandhi's wisdom on lifelong learning, portraying it as a journey of continuous growth.

10. **Conclude with Adaptive Learning as Harmonizing Force:**
    Reinforce adaptive learning as the harmonizing force in leadership's symphony, propelling continual growth and adaptability.

Adaptive learning is the compass of progress, navigating the ever-shifting landscape of challenges and opportunities. Embrace the rhythm of continuous learning, for in its cadence lies the melody of resilience, innovation, and the perpetual dance with the evolving tapestry of knowledge.

—Douglas Pflug

FINAL THOUGHTS

Adaptive Learning:

"Adaptive Leadership Mastery: Navigating Change with Skill and Agility"
In the dynamic landscape of 2025 and beyond, leadership training is a journey into adaptive leadership mastery. Leaders are trained not only to embrace change but to thrive in it. Through adaptive learning training, leaders develop the skills to anticipate, respond, and lead

through uncertainty. Training programs cultivate an adaptive mindset, empowering leaders to turn challenges into opportunities and foster a culture of continuous learning and improvement.

"Future-Ready Leadership: The Art of Adaptive Learning"
Leadership training for 2025 is an exploration of future-ready leadership through the art of adaptive learning. Leaders are equipped with the skills to pivot strategies, learn from experiences, and inspire innovation in the face of evolving challenges. Adaptive learning training programs focus on cultivating resilience, agility, and a proactive approach to change, ensuring leaders are not just prepared for the future but are architects of it.

These messages highlight the crucial role of adaptive learning in leadership training, emphasizing the need for leaders to be agile, resilient, and proactive in navigating the uncertainties of the future.

CHAPTER QUOTES

1. **Charles Darwin**

   It is not the strongest of the species that survive, nor the most intelligent, but the one most responsive to change.
   https://www.goodreads.com/quotes/5538-it-is-not-the-
   strongest-of-the-species-that-survive

2. **Peter Drucker**

   The best way to predict the future is to create it.
   https://www.brainyquote.com/quotes/peter_drucker_120149

3. **Mahatma Gandhi**

   Live as if you were to die tomorrow, learn as if you were to live forever.
   https://www.goodreads.com/quotes/6973-live-as-if-you-
   were-to-die-tomorrow-learn-as

4. **John C. Maxwell**

   The greatest mistake we make is living in constant fear that we will make one.
   https://www.goodreads.com/quotes/184683-the-greatest-
   mistake-we-make-is-living-in-constant-fear

5. **William Pollard**

Learning and innovation go hand in hand. The arrogance of success is to think that what you did yesterday will be sufficient for tomorrow.

https://www.brainyquote.com/quotes/william_
pollard_104985

6. **Alvin Toffler**

The illiterate of the 21st century will not be those who cannot read and write, but those who cannot learn, unlearn, and relearn.

https://ww.goodreads.com/quotes/11509-the-illiterate-
of-the-21st-century-will-not-be-those

Chapter 7

Inclusive "All In" Leadership

FOSTERING DIVERSE AND INCLUSIVE ENVIRONMENTS TO HARNESS THE POWER OF VARIED PERSPECTIVES

Photo Credit: Katrina Wright https://unsplash.com/

> Inclusive leadership is the orchestrator of harmony, weaving a tapestry of diverse voices into a symphony of innovation. By nurturing environments where every perspective is not only heard but celebrated, we unlock the true power of collective wisdom and illuminate the path to a brighter, more inclusive future.
>
> —Douglas Pflug

DOI: 10.1201/9781003518099-10

MY THOUGHTS AND COMMENTARY

Inclusive leadership is the orchestrator of harmony, weaving a tapestry of diverse voices into a symphony of innovation. By nurturing environments where every perspective is not only heard but celebrated, we unlock the true power of collective wisdom and illuminate the path to a brighter, more inclusive future.

I have been extremely fortunate throughout my life to be raised in an inclusive home.

This inclusivity has been a constant thread woven into the fabric of my experiences, from athletics and leadership to my work, coaching, counseling, mentoring, and teaching opportunities. The organizations I have had the pleasure to work with have all been very progressive in terms of diversity, equity, and inclusiveness, and these three principles underpin everything I do.

As we progress into 2025 and beyond, we must continue to prioritize the "H.B." or the "human being" side of things, emphasizing our commonalities rather than our differences. While I deeply appreciate diversity, both personally and professionally, in moments of emergent need, the distinctions between us become inconsequential. What fuels my assistance is the fundamental understanding that another human being requires help.

Some may argue that this perspective does not fully recognize or support DEI (Diversity, Equity, and Inclusion). I would argue that it does so more than ever. In certain elements of society, the emphasis on DEI can inadvertently lead to discrimination against others. The guiding principles I adhere to when leading with DEI and encourage you to are as follows:

Recognition of common humanity

Emphasizing the shared human experience to bridge gaps and foster understanding.

Inclusivity beyond differences

Acknowledging and celebrating diversity, while ensuring inclusivity goes beyond just recognizing differences.

Equitable practices

Promoting fairness and impartiality in all aspects of decision-making and resource distribution.

Elimination of discrimination

Actively working to eliminate discriminatory practices and biases within organizational structures.

Community building

Fostering a sense of community where everyone feels valued, heard, and included.

These principles guide my approach to DEI, aiming not only for diversity but also for a holistic and inclusive environment where each person is treated with dignity and respect.

As we move forward, let us continue to build bridges, break down barriers, and champion a world that values and uplifts every individual, regardless of their background or identity.

WHAT DO HISTORY AND GENERAL RESEARCH ILLUSTRATE TO US?

Introduction: The evolution of leadership and the imperative of inclusivity

In the dynamic evolution of leadership paradigms, inclusivity emerges as a cornerstone, transforming organizational cultures from mere acknowledgment of diversity to a celebration of differences.

This promotes thought into the profound impact of inclusive leadership—a conductor orchestrating a symphony of diverse voices harmonizing to sculpt an innovative and vibrant future. As we stand at the threshold of 2025 and look beyond, the indispensability of inclusive leadership looms large, guiding the way to a future characterized by unity and brilliance.

In the progressive realm of leadership, inclusivity is not merely a choice but an imperative. It functions as the orchestrator of harmony, unlocking the latent power of collective wisdom and steering organizations toward unprecedented heights.

CELEBRATING DIVERSITY: THE OVERTURE TO INCLUSIVE LEADERSHIP

> Diversity is not about how we differ. Diversity is about embracing one another's uniqueness.
>
> —Ola Joseph

Ola Joseph's profound words set the tone for this section, laying the foundation for the understanding that diversity is not a divisive force but a wellspring of unique perspectives.

Within these pages, we navigate the landscape where inclusive leaders not only acknowledge but actively celebrate diversity. This unfurls the tapestry where every voice, with its unique hue, contributes to the richness of the organizational narrative.

Leaders are urged to cultivate environments where differences are not only acknowledged but respected and seamlessly integrated into the decision-making fabric.

In the realm of progressive leadership, Ola Joseph's wisdom echoes loud and clear—embracing uniqueness forms the bedrock of inclusive leadership. Leaders, through their actions, create environments where diversity is not just accepted but genuinely celebrated.

As leaders champion diversity, Verna Myers' profound insight serves as a guiding light—diversity is not merely an invitation to the party, but a call to the dance floor of innovation. Inclusive leaders not only extend invitations to diverse perspectives but ensure that every voice actively takes part in the rhythmic dance of innovation.

NURTURING INCLUSIVE ENVIRONMENTS

> The strength of the team is each member. The strength of each member is the team.
>
> —Phil Jackson

Phil Jackson's metaphorical baton takes center stage in this section, guiding leaders in the creation of an inclusive symphony within their teams.

Here, we explore the multifaceted role of inclusive leaders as conductors, adeptly orchestrating harmony by ensuring that every team member feels not only heard but truly valued. This unearths practical strategies for leaders to foster an inclusive environment, emphasizing the symbiotic relationship between individual strengths and collective success.

In the landscape of progressive leadership, Phil Jackson's insight resonates—a team's strength lies not just in its collective might but in the unique contributions of individual members.

As leaders meticulously orchestrate inclusive environments, Maya Angelou's wisdom serves as a poignant reminder—that diversity, akin to a rich tapestry, enhances the organizational narrative. Inclusive leaders, much like skilled weavers, nurture an environment where every thread, standing for an individual's uniqueness, is not only valued but celebrated.

THE POWER OF COLLECTIVE WISDOM

> If everyone is thinking alike, then somebody isn't thinking.
>
> —George S. Patton

This places George S. Patton's perspective at the forefront, accentuating the intrinsic value of diverse thinking. This intricately explores how inclusive leaders unlock the true power of collective wisdom, fostering an environment where varied perspectives are not merely tolerated but actively looked for.

Leaders are encouraged to embrace dissenting opinions, recognizing them as indispensable catalysts for innovation and sustained growth.

In the realm of progressive leadership, George S. Patton's words resonate as a profound truth—if everyone thinks alike, the innovation potential is still untapped. Inclusive leaders understand that diverse perspectives are the very building blocks of a crescendo of innovation.

As leaders harness the power of collective wisdom, Margaret Mead's wisdom becomes a guiding principle—never doubt that a small group of thoughtful, committed citizens can change the world. Indeed, it is the only thing that ever has. Inclusive leaders grasp the transformative potential of diverse voices when united, acknowledging their pivotal role in driving positive and transformative change.

THE LIGHTED PATH: TOWARD A MORE INCLUSIVE FUTURE

> Diversity is the mix. Inclusion is making the mix work.
> —Andres Tapia

Andres Tapia's succinct perspective encapsulates the essence of this section, emphasizing that inclusion is not just about assembling a diverse mix but ensuring that this mix functions cohesively.

This embarks on a journey to unveil how inclusive leadership illuminates the path to a brighter, more inclusive future. It goes beyond mere buzzwords, delving into the lived experience of a culture where diversity is not only acknowledged but actively integrated.

Leaders are compelled to take intentional steps toward inclusivity, recognizing its pivotal role in organizational resilience, adaptability, and enduring success.

In the realm of progressive leadership, Andres Tapia's words resound—making the diverse mix work seamlessly is the ultimate goal of inclusive leadership.

Leaders become torchbearers, illuminating the path to a more inclusive future by actively weaving diversity into the very fabric of organizational culture.

As leaders stride purposefully toward a more inclusive future, Helen Keller's wisdom becomes a guiding light—the best and most beautiful things in the world cannot be seen or even touched—they must be felt with the heart. Inclusive leaders understand that the beauty of inclusivity is not a mere visual spectacle but an emotionally resonant experience. They craft a workplace culture where the benefits of inclusivity are not only seen but deeply felt, fostering authenticity, and a profound sense of belonging.

PREDICTED TRENDS THAT I SPECULATE FOR 2025 AND BEYOND

While I do not have real-time data, I can provide insights into some trends that I believe as a progressive thinking and forward-moving leader that I feel may impact the field of diversity and inclusion. Keep in mind that these trends may have evolved, and it is essential to refer to the latest research and reports for the most current information.

Emphasis on equity and belonging

Organizations were anticipated to shift from just focusing on diversity and inclusion to a more comprehensive approach that includes equity and a sense of belonging. Ensuring fair treatment and fostering an environment where everyone feels they truly belong were expected to be key priorities.

Data-driven data and inclusion strategies

The use of data analytics to measure and track diversity and inclusion efforts was on the rise. Organizations were expected to leverage data to identify gaps, set benchmarks, and measure the effectiveness of diversity and inclusion initiatives.

Neurodiversity and disability inclusion

A growing recognition of the importance of neurodiversity and disability inclusion was anticipated. Companies were expected to focus on creating more inclusive workplaces for individuals with different cognitive abilities and disabilities.

Intersectionality as a key focus

Companies were expected to pay more attention to intersectionality, acknowledging that individuals hold multiple identities simultaneously. Understanding the unique experiences of individuals with intersecting identities, such as race, gender, and sexual orientation, was anticipated to become a central theme in diversity and inclusion efforts.

Remote and hybrid work inclusion

With an increasing trend toward remote and hybrid work models, organizations were expected to emphasize ensuring that diversity and inclusion efforts extend seamlessly to remote settings. This includes addressing potential disparities in opportunities and experiences for remote and in-office employees.

AI and technology in data and inclusion

The use of artificial intelligence (AI) and technology to reduce bias in hiring processes and promote fair treatment in the workplace was anticipated to grow. Technology is expected to play a role in making diversity and inclusion efforts more effective and data driven.

Global inclusion initiatives

As workplaces become more global, companies are expected to focus on creating strategies that address diversity and inclusion on a global scale. This includes understanding cultural nuances, promoting inclusivity across different regions, and incorporating diverse perspectives in decision-making.

Leadership accountability

Anticipated trends included an increased emphasis on leadership accountability. Companies were expected to hold leaders responsible for driving diversity and inclusion initiatives, with leadership goals tied to performance evaluations.

Employee resource groups evolution

Employee Resource Groups (ERGs) were expected to evolve beyond affinity groups to become more strategic in influencing organizational policies and practices. ERGs were anticipated to play a more active role in shaping company culture.

CONCLUSION

These trends are rooted in my extensive 40-plus years of leadership experience, encompassing various roles as both a leader and follower. Over the decades, I've witnessed the ebb and flow of leadership paradigms, shaped by the dynamic interplay of societal shifts, technological advancements, and evolving organizational needs.

The fluidity of leadership trends results from meticulous projections and observations, capturing the dynamic nature of the evolving leadership landscape. With each passing year, new challenges arise, demanding innovative approaches and adaptive leadership styles. It's a testament to the resilience and agility required to thrive in today's rapidly changing world.

Witnessing diversity and inclusiveness enhancing leadership across all facets of life in 2025 and beyond is indeed exciting. Inclusive leadership isn't just a buzzword; it's a paradigm shift toward recognizing and embracing the unique contributions of individuals from all backgrounds. It's about creating environments where every voice is heard, valued, and empowered to contribute to collective success.

In conclusion, inclusive leadership emerges as the orchestrator of harmony, weaving a complex yet harmonious symphony of diverse voices into a seamless fabric of innovation. As leaders navigate the intricate notes of leadership in 2025 and beyond, embracing inclusivity becomes not only a strategic imperative but a transformative force within the grand progressive thinking and forward-moving framework of leadership.

Inclusive leaders are active participants, contributing unique melodies to the harmonious blend propelling organizations toward a future that is not only brighter but inherently more inclusive. They recognize the power of diversity in driving creativity, fostering collaboration, and driving sustainable growth.

This culminates by underscoring the enduring impact of inclusive leadership, highlighting its potential to shape organizational dynamics and redefine the very fabric of leadership in an ever-evolving landscape. Leaders are positioned not just as figureheads but as active contributors to the symphony, their unique melodies playing an integral role in creating a harmonious, inclusive future. As we move forward, let us embrace inclusivity as a cornerstone of leadership excellence, unlocking the full potential of individuals and organizations alike.

CHAPTER "TO-DO" CHECKLIST

1. **Show Inclusive Leadership as an Imperative:**
   Illuminate inclusive leadership as a necessity, essential for harmony and collective wisdom.

2. **Embrace and Celebrate Diversity:**
   Communicate the importance of embracing and celebrating diversity within the organization.

3. **Promote Inclusive Environments through Leadership:**
Portray leaders as conductors guiding inclusive environments, inspired by Phil Jackson's wisdom.

4. **Value Every Thread in the Tapestry:**
Reinforce the concept of valuing and celebrating every individual thread of diversity, echoing Maya Angelou's perspective.

5. **Unlock Collective Wisdom for Innovation:**
Highlight the role of inclusive leaders in unlocking collective wisdom for innovation, inspired by George S. Patton.

6. **Encourage Dissenting Opinions for Growth:**
Position inclusive leaders as catalysts for growth by encouraging dissenting opinions.

7. **Harness the Power of Collective Voices:**
Illustrate the transformative potential of diverse voices when united, inspired by Margaret Mead.

8. **Make Diversity Work Cohesively:**
Emphasize the goal of making diversity work cohesively, echoing Andres Tapia's perspective.

9. **Take Intentional Steps toward Inclusivity:**
Encourage leaders to take intentional steps toward inclusivity for organizational resilience and long-term success.

10. **Create a Workplace Culture of Authenticity and Belonging:**
Foster a culture where inclusivity is deeply felt, resonating with authenticity, and belonging, inspired by Helen Keller's wisdom.

FINAL THOUGHTS

Inclusive leadership

"Inclusive Leadership Excellence: Training Tomorrow's Visionary Leaders"
In the inclusive landscape of 2025 and beyond, leadership training is an immersive experience in inclusive leadership excellence. Leaders are trained not only to embrace diversity but to leverage it as a strategic advantage. Through inclusive leadership training, leaders learn to create environments where every voice is heard, valued, and actively included. Training programs instill the skills to champion diversity, foster a sense of belonging, and drive innovation through a multitude of perspectives.

"Leading beyond Differences: Inclusive Leadership Training for the Future"
Leadership training for 2025 is about leading beyond differences. Inclusive leadership skills become indispensable, and training programs focus on equipping leaders with the tools to understand, appreciate, and leverage diversity. Leaders learn to dismantle barriers, address unconscious biases, and create a culture of inclusivity that goes beyond compliance, unlocking the full potential of diverse teams.

These messages underscore the significance of inclusive leadership in the evolving landscape, emphasizing the need for leaders to not only value diversity but actively lead in ways that foster inclusion, belonging, and innovation.

CHAPTER QUOTES

1. Maya Angelou

   That diversity, akin to a rich tapestry, enhances the organizational narrative.
   https://www.brainyquote.com/quotes/maya_angelou_133420

2. Phil Jackson

   The strength of the team is each member. The strength of each member is the team.
   https://www.brainyquote.com/quotes/phil_jackson_210184

3. Ola Joseph

   Diversity is not about how we differ. Diversity is about embracing one another's uniqueness.
   https://www.goodreads.com/quotes/9511558-we-choose-between-descriptions-of-options-rather-than-between-the

4. Margaret Mead

Never doubt that a small group of thoughtful, committed citizens can change the world. Indeed, it is the only thing that ever has.
    https://www.brainyquote.com/quotes/margaret_mead_121718

5. Verna Myers

Diversity is not merely an invitation to the party, but a call to the dance floor of innovation.
    https://www.brainyquote.com/quotes/verna_myers_1003198

6. George S. Patton

If everyone is thinking alike, then somebody isn't thinking.
    https://www.brainyquote.com/quotes/george_s_patton_102991

7. Andres Tapia

Diversity is the mix. Inclusion is making the mix work.
    https://www.goodreads.com/quotes/576505-diversity-is-
    the-mix-inclusion-is-making-the-mix-work

Inclusive leadership is the orchestrator of harmony, weaving a tapestry of diverse voices into a symphony of innovation. By nurturing environments where every perspective is not only heard but celebrated, we unlock the true power of collective wisdom and illuminate the path to a brighter, more inclusive future.

—Douglas Pflug

Chapter 8

Resilience Cultivation

**BUILDING RESILIENCE TO NAVIGATE UNCERTAINTIES
AND SETBACKS WITH A POSITIVE MINDSET**

Photo Credit: Fab Lentz https://unsplash.com/

Resilience cultivation is the art of growing stronger in the face of storms, a testament to the human spirit's ability to bloom amidst challenges. Plant the seeds of a positive mindset, water them with perseverance, and watch as the garden of resilience flourishes, turning setbacks into steppingstones on the path to triumph.

—Douglas Pflug

DOI: 10.1201/9781003518099-11

MY THOUGHTS AND COMMENTARY

Authenticity in leadership is the beacon that lights the way for meaningful connections. When leaders embrace their genuine selves with transparency and sincerity, they forge a profound bond that transcends titles. In the symphony of leadership, authenticity is the melody that resonates in the hearts of those who follow, creating a harmonious and impactful journey together.

In 2022, I wrote and published *Finding Your Granite: My Four Cornerstones of Personal Leadership*,[1] with the overarching theme centered on the resilience cultivated through positive and negative lessons learned, failures, and growth.

To best illustrate what resilience means to me and its roots within me, I would like to share an excerpt from Chapter #1 titled "That little sucker wouldn't die."

In my leadership courses, I prompt participants to engage in a reflective exercise contemplating their past, present, and future selves. I guide discussions by initiating a dialogue with a thought-provoking statement:

The person you once were no longer exists, yet it shapes who you are today.

The person you are today is transient, giving way to the individual you aspire to become tomorrow.

Finding Your Granite: Chapter #1 (Edited)

"That little sucker wouldn't die."

I was born on September 23, 1966, "just an average baby" in Stratford, Ontario, to Paul and Joan Pflug. Despite not being born into wealth or possessing exceptional athletic or intellectual gifts, my life took an unexpected turn shortly after birth. Diagnosed with Pyloric Stenosis, my parents faced the prospect of losing me, but life-saving surgery proved successful, leaving me with a 12-inch scar as a daily reminder of that critical moment.

Around the age of three, another challenge emerged as I was diagnosed with Immune thrombocytopenia (ITP). Uncertainty loomed, and once again, my parents were told to prepare for the worst. My mother, Joan, vividly recalls those trying times, when prayers and medical interventions became the lifeline for my survival.

A poignant childhood story involving illness and faith left an indelible mark on me. It instilled an irrational fear of sleeping with my arms outstretched, a minor comfort-turned-fear that persisted for years.

Fast forward several years, sitting by a cottage fire with my father; he shared the fear and helplessness he felt during those early years of my life.

His prayers and private struggles were a testament to the gravity of the situation. His relief and joy upon hearing I would survive were encapsulated in his triumphant exclamation, "This little sucker does not want to die."

Reflecting on my childhood, I sensed a greater purpose and calling in life. As a Christian, I believe in an afterlife where judgment awaits, and I am confident that the doctors who saved me continue to watch over me as guardian angels.

Despite a lingering "why me?" questioning my early existence, I embraced life with urgency, believing that every moment should be lived to the fullest. Childhood adversity, I now realize, was a precursor to building resilience for greater challenges ahead.

In my prior research on childhood trauma and resilience, I came across an article titled "Resilience in children: strategies to strengthen your kids." It resonated with my own experiences, reinforcing my belief that those caring doctors saved my life for a purpose beyond their immediate actions. I credit my parents for instilling a "never say die" attitude and implementing practices that would serve as a foundation for resilience in the years to come.

Thanks, Mom and Dad

I hope that this chapter excerpt and the book in general offer you valuable insights that may resonate with your personal and professional "granite" as you navigate 2025 and beyond.

Note: I am immensely pleased with the outcomes of this project, as it allowed me to confront my own PTSD demons and share my story with other first responders who may be silently suffering. Knowing that I played a role in saving lives through this process brings me profound joy, as it signifies that my pain can be a source of strength for others in their recovery.

Another aspect of this project that fills me with pride is the decision to donate 100% of the book sales to www.v-eh.ca, contributing to the charity's efforts to provide service dogs for wounded front-line workers. Inspired by the wise words of Mr. Stu Lang, a great mentor I have followed for years, who always emphasized that "it's up to each man to give, you just have to find out how you can give." I hope that my contributions have honored Coach Lang's legacy of incredible leadership, which has cultivated the leadership skills of thousands of people privileged to know him.

WHAT DO HISTORY AND GENERAL RESEARCH ILLUSTRATE TO US?

Resilience cultivation: Growing stronger amid storms

Resilience cultivation is an art, a testament to the human spirit's ability to bloom amid challenges. Planting the seeds of a positive mindset, and watering them with perseverance, we see the garden of resilience flourishing. Setbacks become steppingstones on the path to triumph, illustrating the transformative power of resilience in navigating life's storms.

The only limit to our realization of tomorrow will be our doubts of today.

—Franklin D. Roosevelt

This section expands on the metaphor of resilience as a garden, exploring the role of positive mindset and perseverance. The quote by Franklin D. Roosevelt sets the tone for embracing resilience as a force that transcends doubts and limitations.

RESILIENCY: HOW TO OVERCOME CHAOS

It's not that I'm so smart, it's just that I stay with problems longer.

—Albert Einstein

Out of difficulties grow miracles.

—Jean de La Bruyère

Resilience is a complex trait that involves the ability to bounce back from adversity, navigate challenges, and adapt positively to stress or trauma. Here are some key characteristics and skills associated with resilient individuals:

AUTHOR'S SUGGESTED KEYS FOR SUCCESS

Positive outlook

Resilient individuals tend to support a positive outlook, focusing on solutions rather than problems. They often see challenges as opportunities for growth.

Self-awareness

Being aware of one's emotions, thoughts, and reactions is crucial for resilience. Self-aware individuals can better understand their strengths and limitations.

Adaptability

Resilient people are adaptable and can adjust to new circumstances. They view change as a natural part of life and are willing to adjust their goals and plans accordingly.

Strong social connections

Building and supporting supportive relationships is a key factor in resilience. Having a strong social support system supplies emotional aid during tough times.

Critical thinking skills

Resilient individuals are effective analytical people. They approach challenges with a solution-oriented mindset, breaking down problems into manageable parts.

Emotional regulation

The ability to manage and regulate emotions is crucial for resilience. Resilient individuals can navigate through negative emotions and keep composure in stressful situations.

Optimism and hope

An optimistic outlook enables resilient individuals to see hope. This positive mindset helps them persevere through tough times.

Self-efficacy

Resilient people have a belief in their ability to manage challenges and influence their outcomes. This sense of self-efficacy empowers them to act in the face of adversity.

Flexibility

Flexibility in thinking and behavior allows resilient individuals to adjust their strategies when faced with setbacks. They are open to different perspectives and approaches.

Initiative-taking for coping

Rather than waiting for problems to escalate, resilient individuals take initiative-taking steps to cope with stress. This might involve seeking social support, engaging in self-care, or seeking professional help.

Sense of purpose

A clear sense of purpose and direction in life can contribute to resilience. Having goals and aspirations supplies motivation during challenging times.

Mindfulness and acceptance

Mindfulness practices and acceptance of the present moment contribute to resilience. Being able to stay grounded in the present helps individuals manage stress and anxiety.

Learning from experiences

Resilient individuals view challenges as opportunities for learning and personal growth. They extract lessons from difficult experiences that contribute to their development.

It is important to note that resilience is a dynamic and evolving trait, and individuals may develop these characteristics over time through various life experiences and coping mechanisms. Additionally, seeking professional support, such as therapy, can be beneficial for building resilience.

INTRODUCTION: THE RESONANCE OF AUTHENTIC LEADERSHIP

In the ever-evolving landscape of leadership, authenticity emerges as a guiding force, shaping a symphony that transcends traditional paradigms. This explores the profound impact of authenticity—the authentic leader as a beacon illuminating the path toward meaningful connections.

As leaders navigate the complexities of 2025 and beyond, authenticity becomes the resonant melody that binds teams and leaders in a harmonious and impactful journey.

In progressive thinking and forward-moving leadership, authenticity is not merely a trait; it is the resonant melody that binds leaders and teams in a harmonious and impactful journey.

> The most common way people give up their power is by thinking they don't have any.
>
> —Alice Walker

Alice Walker's quote deepens the understanding of authenticity as a source of personal power. It encourages leaders to recognize and embrace their inherent power, aligning with the theme of authenticity in leadership.

AUTHENTICITY AS A LEADERSHIP BEACON: ILLUMINATING THE PATH

> To be yourself in a world that is constantly trying to make you something else is the greatest accomplishment.
>
> —Ralph Waldo Emerson

Ralph Waldo Emerson's timeless wisdom sets the tone for understanding the profound essence of authenticity in leadership.

This explores authenticity as a beacon—a guiding light that illuminates the path for leaders to be true to themselves amid external pressures.

Leaders are encouraged to embrace their unique identity, fostering a workplace culture that values individuality and diversity of thought.

In progressive thinking and forward-moving leadership, Ralph Waldo Emerson's words echo—that the greatest accomplishment is to be oneself. Authentic leaders illuminate the path for others, creating a workplace culture that celebrates individuality.

> The only way to do great work is to love what you do.
> —Steve Jobs

Steve Jobs' quote introduces the idea that authenticity is intertwined with passion and genuine love for one's work. It reinforces the importance of embracing one's true self in the pursuit of great accomplishments.

TRANSPARENCY AND SINCERITY: THE BUILDING BLOCKS OF AUTHENTIC BONDS

> The strength of a nation derives from the integrity of the home.
> —Confucius

Confucius' profound insight extends beyond the home to the realm of leadership.

This promotes thought into transparency and sincerity as the building blocks of authentic bonds.

Leaders are encouraged to cultivate an environment where integrity is the bedrock, fostering trust and openness among team members. This explores practical strategies for leaders to embody transparency and sincerity, creating a workplace culture that values authenticity in communication and decision-making.

In progressive thinking and forward-moving leadership, Confucius' wisdom resonates—the strength of a team derives from the integrity of its leaders. Authentic bonds are forged through transparency and sincerity, creating a harmonious and impactful journey together.

> I am not afraid of storms, for I am learning how to sail my ship.
> —Louisa May Alcott

Louisa May Alcott's quote becomes a metaphorical anchor, emphasizing that authenticity is not about avoiding challenges but learning to navigate and grow from them. It reinforces the idea that authenticity is about resilience in the face of storms.

FORGING PROFOUND BONDS: AUTHENTICITY BEYOND TITLES

> Authenticity is a collection of choices that we have to make every day. It is about the choice to show up and be real. The choice to be honest. The choice to let our true selves be seen.
>
> —Brené Brown

Brené Brown's insightful perspective forms the crux of this section, emphasizing authenticity as a daily choice. Leaders are urged to go beyond the confines of titles, revealing their true selves to foster profound connections. This explores the impact of authentic leadership on team dynamics, innovation, and overall organizational culture.

In progressive thinking and forward-moving leadership, Brené Brown's words resonate—authenticity is a daily choice that transcends titles, fostering profound bonds that elevate team dynamics and organizational culture.

> Success is not final, failure is not fatal: It is the courage to continue that count.
>
> —Winston Churchill

Winston Churchill's quote adds a dimension of courage to authenticity, emphasizing that the journey of being authentic is ongoing. It encourages leaders to find strength in their authenticity, even in the face of challenges.

THE PRESENCE OF AUTHENTICITY: RESONATING IN THE HEARTS OF FOLLOWERS

> To be yourself in a world that is constantly trying to make you something else is the greatest accomplishment.
>
> —Ralph Waldo Emerson

Returning to Ralph Waldo Emerson's profound words, this reinforces the central theme—the greatest accomplishment is to be oneself.

Authentic leaders create a resonant melody in the symphony of leadership, one that echoes in the hearts of those who follow. This explores the impact of authenticity on employee engagement, loyalty, and overall job satisfaction.

In progressive thinking and forward-moving leadership, Ralph Waldo Emerson's words echo—that the greatest accomplishment is to be oneself.

Authentic leaders create a resonant melody that resonates in the hearts of those who follow.

The best way to predict the future is to create it.

—Peter Drucker

Peter Drucker's quote emphasizes the forward-looking aspect of authenticity. It encourages leaders to shape their future by being true to themselves, creating a narrative that aligns with their authentic values.

CONCLUSION: THE HARMONIOUS AND IMPACTFUL JOURNEY OF AUTHENTIC LEADERSHIP

In conclusion, authenticity in leadership emerges as the beacon that lights the way for meaningful connections. In the symphony of leadership, authenticity is not a mere trait; it is the resonant melody that transcends titles, fostering a harmonious and impactful journey together.

As leaders navigate the complexities of 2025 and beyond, embracing authenticity becomes not only a leadership style but a transformative force that resonates in the hearts of those who follow, creating a legacy of genuine connection and impactful leadership.

This highlights the enduring impact of authentic leadership, emphasizing its potential to shape not just organizational dynamics but the very fabric of leadership in the evolving landscape.

Leaders are encouraged to see authenticity as a journey—one that not only enriches their own experience but creates a harmonious and impactful symphony for those they lead.

CHAPTER "TO-DO" CHECKLIST

1. **Position Authenticity as a Guiding Melody:**
   Communicate authenticity not as a trait but as the guiding melody in the symphony of leadership, emphasizing its transformative power.

2. **Illuminate the Path through Authentic Leadership:**
   Use Ralph Waldo Emerson's wisdom to convey authenticity as a beacon, illuminating the path for leaders to be true to themselves amid external pressures.

3. **Highlight Transparency and Sincerity as Foundations:**
   Emphasize Confucius' insight, highlighting transparency and sincerity as the building blocks of authentic bonds and the strength of a team.

4. **Encourage Daily Choices for Authenticity**:
   Introduce Brené Brown's perspective to underscore authenticity as a daily choice, urging leaders to go beyond titles and be real and honest.

5. **Explore the Impact beyond Titles**:
   Build on Brené Brown's concept by delving into authenticity's impact on team dynamics, innovation, and overall organizational culture, emphasizing its transformative potential.

6. **Reinforce Authenticity as a Daily Choice**:
   Reiterate Brené Brown's concept, emphasizing that authenticity is not just a trait but a daily choice that fosters profound bonds beyond professional titles.

7. **Illustrate the Emotional Impact on Followers**:
   Return to Ralph Waldo Emerson's words to highlight the emotional impact of authenticity on followers, resonating in their hearts and contributing to engagement and loyalty.

8. **Emphasize Authentic Leadership as a Source of Inspiration**:
   Introduce Steve Jobs' wisdom to underscore the influential role of personal example in authentic leadership, inspiring others to embrace their genuine selves.

9. **Position Authenticity as a Transformative Force**:
   Conclude with Mahatma Gandhi's perspective, encouraging leaders to see authenticity as a journey and a transformative force that creates a harmonious and impactful symphony.

10. **Highlight Authentic Leadership's Enduring Impact**:
    Close this by emphasizing the enduring impact of authentic leadership, shaping not just organizational dynamics but the very fabric of leadership in the evolving landscape.

FINAL THOUGHTS

Resiliency Cultivation

"Resilient Leadership Mastery: Training Leaders for Adversity and Growth"
In the resilient landscape of 2025 and beyond, leadership training is a transformative journey into resilient leadership mastery. Leaders are trained not only to weather storms but to thrive in adversity. Through resiliency cultivation training, leaders develop the skills to bounce forward from setbacks, foster adaptive thinking, and instill a culture of perseverance within their teams. Training programs empower leaders to view challenges not as obstacles but as opportunities for growth and transformation.

"Leadership for the Long Haul: Resiliency Cultivation in a Dynamic World"
Leadership training for 2025 is about preparing leaders for the long haul through resiliency cultivation. Leaders learn to navigate uncertainty, manage stress, and inspire resilience in their teams. Resiliency cultivation training programs focus on developing emotional intelligence, coping strategies, and a positive mindset, ensuring that leaders not only endure challenges but emerge stronger, fostering a culture of sustained success.

These messages underscore the critical role of resiliency cultivation in leadership training, emphasizing the need for leaders to be equipped with the skills to navigate uncertainties and inspire resilience within their teams.

CHAPTER QUOTES

1. **Louisa May Alcott**

   "I am not afraid of storms, for I am learning how to sail my ship."
   https://www.goodreads.com/quotes/9434-i-am-not-afraid-of-storms-for-i-am

2. **Brené Brown**

   "Vulnerability is the birthplace of connection."
   https://www.brainyquote.com/quotes/brene_brown_819166

3. **Jean de La Bruyère**

   "Out of difficulties grow miracles."
   https://www.goodreads.com/quotes/156947-out-of-difficulties-grow-miracles

4. **Winston Churchill**

Success is not final, failure is not fatal: It is the courage to continue that count.

> https://www.goodreads.com/quotes/6893695-success-is-not-final-failure-is-not-fatal-it-is

5. **Confucius**

The strength of a nation derives from the integrity of the home.

> https://www.brainyquote.com/quotes/confucius_100998

6. **Peter Drucker**

The best way to predict the future is to create it.

> https://www.brainyquote.com/quotes/peter_drucker_118188

7. **Ralph Waldo Emerson**

To be yourself in a world that is constantly trying to make you something else is the greatest accomplishment.

> https://www.brainyquote.com/quotes/ralph_waldo_emerson_106108

8. **Albert Einstein**

It's not that I'm so smart, it's just that I stay with problems longer.

> https://www.brainyquote.com/quotes/albert_einstein_131187

9. **Steve Jobs**

Your time is limited, don't waste it living someone else's life.

> https://www.brainyquote.com/quotes/steve_jobs_416689

10. **Franklin D. Roosevelt**

The only limit to our realization of tomorrow will be our doubts of today.

> https://www.brainyquote.com/quotes/franklin_d_roosevelt_400696

11. **Alice Walker**

The most common way people give up their power is by thinking they don't have any.

> https://www.goodreads.com/quotes/10674-the-most-common-way-people-give-up-their-power-is

Resilience cultivation is the art of growing stronger in the face of storms, a testament to the human spirit's ability to bloom amidst challenges. Plant the seeds of a positive mindset, water them with perseverance, and watch as the garden of resilience flourishes, turning setbacks into steppingstones on the path to triumph.

—Douglas Pflug

NOTE

1 https://www.taylorfrancis.com/books/mono/10.1201/9781003187189/ finding-granite-douglas-pflug.

Part 3

Ensuring Sustainability and Continued Optimization

Photo credit: Zbynek Burivalasey https://unsplash.com

As we stride into the era of personal leadership in 2025 and beyond, let's cultivate a legacy of sustainability. Nurturing our growth with mindful choices and resilience ensures not only our success but also the enduring prosperity of our personal leadership journey, leaving a positive impact for generations to come.

—Douglas Pflug

DOI: 10.1201/9781003518099-12

Chapter 9

Human-Centric Leadership in the Digital Age

BALANCING TECHNOLOGY AND WELL-BEING

Photo Credit: Jeremy Beck https://unsplash.com/

Human-centric technology is the bridge between innovation and empathy, where the advancement of tools and systems is harmoniously entwined with the well-being and connections of individuals. In this symbiotic dance, we don't just create technology; we craft experiences that elevate humanity, ensuring our digital evolution remains a reflection of our shared values and collective aspirations.

—Douglas Pflug

DOI: 10.1201/9781003518099-13

MY THOUGHTS AND COMMENTARY

Human-centric technology is the bridge between innovation and empathy, where the advancement of tools and systems is harmoniously entwined with the well-being and connections of individuals. In this symbiotic dance, we don't just create technology; we craft experiences that elevate humanity, ensuring our digital evolution remains a reflection of our shared values and collective aspirations.

So, there I was, doing my leadership instructor role a few weeks back, casually dropping references to "Leave It to Beaver" during a lecture. Cue blank stares from the students. Undeterred, I smoothly transitioned into a tale from my law enforcement days when I had to find a pay phone to call the desk sergeant. More blank stares. The grand finale? I mentioned a VHS tape, and the class erupted in laughter. Yeah, I am a relic from a bygone era, when pay phones and VHS tapes were a thing.

Now, let me tell you about my high-tech misadventure at my teaching job. I found this article on technology bridging innovation, empathy, and human connection, and it got me thinking about the good old days. Back then, technology was more like a distant cousin at a family reunion—rarely seen and not that important.

Flashback to when I started teaching and had a printer setup issue. In a fit of desperation, I shot a message to our IT guy, all caps,

HEY GUYS, CAN YOU HELP ME? MY COMPUTER PRINTER SETUP ISN'T WORKING?

Little did I know, the mighty power of caps lock would set off an IT emergency.

Within minutes, I heard thunderous footsteps charging down the hallway toward me. I stood up, ready for action, only to be met by a panting IT staff member at my door.

Confused, I asked what the commotion was about. He, still catching his breath, accused me of yelling at him.

Turns out, that using all caps is the digital equivalent of a scream.

Who knew? I got a good laugh and a crash course in internet etiquette. Ah, the joys of being a tech-savvy relic in a digital world.

What a great lesson to learn: "Tech bridges innovation, empathy, and human connection."

Before the lockdowns, much like everyone, we had a busy social schedule, and when COVID hit, we were all locked down and "socially paralyzed."

While the COVID lockdown presented significant challenges, some couples found unexpected benefits in socializing with other couples during this time. Here are three potential advantages:

ENHANCED QUALITY TIME

The lockdown encouraged couples to spend more quality time together. With fewer external commitments and distractions, couples had the opportunity to engage in meaningful conversations, shared activities, and bonding experiences.

CREATIVE VIRTUAL SOCIALIZING

The restrictions prompted couples to explore creative ways to socialize with other couples virtually. Online game nights, virtual dinners, and video calls became popular alternatives to traditional in-person gatherings. This not only maintained social connections but also provided a chance to interact with a broader network of friends and couples, regardless of geographical distances.

One Saturday night, we had three one-hour mini-dates with three different couples. That was amazing because we had been trying to see them for ages, and this way, we were able to spend meaningful time with all three couples.

Professionally, we need to maximize what we gain through *Creative Virtual Socializing* and have far greater coaching, counselling, and mentoring sessions in the "mini dates" spirit with my employees to increase our presence in their lives and assist them in realizing their professional dreams, goals, or desires.

SHARED CHALLENGES AND SUPPORTIVE EXERCISES

We must also incorporate these "mini dates" to assist in *Shared Challenges and Supportive exercises with our colleagues.*

This is extremely important when we have migrated to a hybrid home/office workstyle so we can deal with the uncertainties and stressors of the pandemic and become a shared experience for many couples. This common challenge fostered a sense of solidarity and mutual support. Engaging with other couples allowed for the exchange of coping strategies, advice, and emotional support. Couples found comfort in knowing they were not alone in navigating the unique difficulties posed by the lockdown.

To be progressive in our thought processes and forward-moving leaders, we need to stay current with the best practices that are being utilized across all industries.

Take them, tweak them, make them your own and be successful.

—Douglas Pflug

WHAT DO HISTORY AND GENERAL RESEARCH ILLUSTRATE TO US?

Introduction: The nuances of technology in leadership

The advent of technology in leadership requires a nuanced understanding that goes beyond mere innovation.

The essence lies in recognizing that technology is not an end but a means to elevate human experiences. Human-centric technology serves as the compass, guiding leaders in creating a digital ecosystem that resonates with shared values. In this nuanced landscape, leaders navigate beyond the surface of technological advancements, delving into the depths of how these innovations can enhance the human experience.

Leaders are urged to understand that the true power of technology lies not just in its capabilities but in the way it can be wielded to prioritize the well-being and collaboration of individuals. As they embrace this understanding, leaders emerge as architects of a digital landscape where the focus is not solely on the tools but on how those tools can be wielded to enhance the human experience.

In the progressive tapestry of leadership, Bill Gates' perspective becomes the cornerstone—an insightful reminder that technology is just a tool, and the teacher, or in this case, the leader is the most important. Leaders, armed with this understanding, embark on a journey to orchestrate technology in a way that prioritizes collaboration, motivation, and the collective growth of individuals.

The computer was born to solve problems that did not exist before.

—Bill Gates

As leaders understand human-centric technology, the words of Steve Jobs become a guiding principle—technology is nothing. What is important is having faith in people and recognizing that they are inherently good and smart. When given the right tools, they can perform wonders. Understanding human-centric technology is about acknowledging the centrality of human agency and values in the digital landscape.

Technology is nothing. What's important is that you have faith in people, that they're good and smart, and if you give them tools, they'll do wonderful things with them.

—Steve Jobs

CRAFTING EXPERIENCES THAT ELEVATE HUMANITY

In the symphony of human-centric technology, crafting experiences becomes the heartbeat of innovation. It transcends the realm of prediction, urging leaders not only to foresee the future but actively take part in its creation. Peter Drucker's wisdom echoes through this movement, setting the stage for leaders to become architects of a digital future where technology is not merely innovative but designed to enhance the well-being of individuals and create meaningful connections.

The crafting of experiences that elevate humanity involves initiative-taking leadership, where leaders actively shape the future rather than passively adapt to it. It is a call to become digital storytellers, weaving narratives where technology is not just a tool but a catalyst for positive change.

In this realm, Mark Zuckerberg's words become a guiding light—the biggest risk is not taking any risk. Crafting experiences that elevate humanity involves taking calculated risks, pushing boundaries, and envisioning a future that reflects our collective aspirations.

The biggest risk is not taking any risk. In a world that's changing quickly, the only strategy that is guaranteed to fail is not taking risks.

—Mark Zuckerberg

Leaders, as architects of the digital future, embark on a journey to create a narrative where technology is seamlessly integrated into the human experience, enhancing our lives, and fostering meaningful connections.

Human-centric technology calls leaders to step into the role of visionaries, where the act of crafting experiences becomes a testament to their commitment to elevating humanity.

FOSTERING A CULTURE OF COLLECTIVE ASPIRATIONS

In the evolving narrative of human-centric technology, fostering a culture where collective aspirations shape the use of technology takes center stage. Peter Drucker's words guide leaders to unite values and technology, leveraging the power of digital tools to transcend physical barriers and enhance communication.

The true power of human-centric technology is realized in a culture where collective aspirations guide the use of digital tools.

Technology becomes a unifying force, transcending geographical boundaries and cultural differences. Fostering a culture of collective aspirations involves aligning technological advancements with the values and goals shared by a diverse community. Leaders become navigators in this cultural landscape, ensuring that technology is not a divisive force but a cohesive one, connecting people and amplifying their voices.

Satya Nadella's principle becomes the compass in this movement—the most exciting thing about the digital revolution is the democratization of opportunity. In a culture shaped by human-centric technology, opportunities are not confined; they are democratized, ensuring that the benefits of technology are accessible to all.

> The most exciting thing about the digital revolution is the democratization of opportunity.
>
> —Satya Nadella

Leaders, as custodians of this culture, become champions of inclusivity, where the digital revolution becomes a vehicle for empowering individuals and communities.

CONCLUSION: SHAPING THE LEGACY OF HUMAN-CENTRIC TECHNOLOGY

As human-centric technology reaches its crescendo, leaders find themselves at the precipice of shaping a legacy in 2025 and beyond. The interconnected movements of understanding human centricity, crafting experiences that elevate humanity, and fostering a culture of collective aspirations create a rhythm that enriches lives and positively affects organizations.

In the dynamic intersection of leadership and technology, leaders can create a legacy where the evolution of digital tools aligns seamlessly with the values and aspirations of a collective humanity.

The symphony of human-centric technology is not just a concept; it is a legacy in the making. The nuances of technology in leadership, the crafting of experiences, and the fostering of a culture of collective aspirations become the brushstrokes that paint this legacy.

As leaders navigate the digital landscape with a focus on human well-being and values, they shape a legacy of innovation, collaboration, and a meaningful connection between humanity and technology.

Human-centric technology is not a mere melody; it is an opus in which leaders are both composers and conductors, shaping the narrative of a future where technology elevates humanity and reflects our shared aspirations.

CHAPTER "TO-DO" CHECKLIST

1. **Define Human-Centric Technology:**
   Clearly articulate human-centric technology as the bridge between innovation and empathy, emphasizing its role in enhancing well-being and connections.

2. **Highlight Human-Centricity as a Guiding Principle:**
   Position human-centricity as the guiding principle for leaders crafting meaningful digital experiences, ensuring technology aligns with shared values and aspirations.

3. **Understand Technology as a Tool:**
   Use Bill Gates' insight to show a foundational understanding that technology is a tool, emphasizing the pivotal role of leaders in wielding it for collaboration and motivation.

4. **Orchestrate Technology Use for Collaboration:**
   Emphasize the role of leaders in orchestrating technology use to foster collaboration, motivation, and a shared sense of purpose among individuals.

5. **Craft Experiences That Elevate Humanity:**
   Integrate Peter Drucker's wisdom to guide leaders in crafting experiences that not only embrace innovation but elevate the human experience.

6. **Actively Shape the Future:**
   Encourage initiative-taking leadership by heeding Peter Drucker's perspective, urging leaders to actively shape the digital future rather than passively adapting to it.

7. **Align Technology with Collective Aspirations:**
   Unite values and technology by leveraging Peter Drucker's words, fostering a culture where collective aspirations guide the use of digital tools.

8. **Use Technology to Transcend Barriers:**
   Highlight the potential of technology, as emphasized by Peter Drucker, to cut physical costs of communication and transcend geographical barriers.

9. **Democratize Opportunity through Technology:**
   Embrace Satya Nadella's principle to foster a culture of collective aspirations, ensuring the democratization of opportunities in the digital revolution.

10. **Create a Legacy of Innovation and Connection:**
Conclude by positioning the symphony of human-centric technology as a legacy that leaders can shape, enriching lives, positively changing organizations, and creating a meaningful connection between humanity and technology.

FINAL THOUGHTS

Human-Centric Leadership in a Digital Age:

"Human-Centric Leadership Excellence: Training Leaders for the Digital Frontier."
In the digitally infused landscape of 2025 and beyond, leadership training is a transformative experience in human-centric leadership excellence. Leaders are trained not only to harness technology but to put humanity at the forefront of their leadership. Through human-centric leadership training, leaders gain the skills to understand, connect with, and inspire their teams in a digital world. Training programs empower leaders to create workplaces where technology augments human potential, fostering a culture of empathy, collaboration, and individual growth.

"Leading with Heart in a Digital World: Human-Centric Leadership Training"
Leadership training for 2025 is about leading with heart in a digital world. Human-centric leadership skills become indispensable, and training programs focus on equipping leaders with the tools to balance technological advancements with human needs. Leaders learn to prioritize employee well-being, create meaningful connections, and foster a sense of purpose in a digitally driven work environment.

These messages underscore the importance of human-centric leadership in the digital age, emphasizing the need for leaders to blend technological advancements with a deep understanding and appreciation of the human experience.

CHAPTER QUOTES

1. **Bill Gates**

   The computer was born to solve problems that did not exist before.
   https://www.brainyquote.com/quotes/bill_gates_121113

2. **Satya Nadella**

   The most exciting thing about the digital revolution is the democratization of opportunity.
   https://www.brainyquote.com/quotes/satya_nadella_997929

3. **Steve Jobs**

   -Technology is nothing. What's important is that you have faith in people, that they're good and smart, and if you give them tools, they'll do wonderful things with them.
   https://www.goodreads.com/quotes/24530-technology-is-nothing-what-s-important-is-that-you-have

4. **Mark Zuckerberg**

   The biggest risk is not taking any risk. In a world that's changing quickly, the only strategy that is guaranteed to fail is not taking risks.
   https://www.brainyquote.com/quotes/mark_zuckerberg_842701

   Human-centric technology is the bridge between innovation and empathy, where the advancement of tools and systems is harmoniously entwined with the well-being and connections of individuals. In this symbiotic dance, we don't just create technology; we craft experiences that elevate humanity, ensuring our digital evolution remains a reflection of our shared values and collective aspirations.
   —Douglas Pflug

Chapter 10

The Heart of Leadership

A DEEP DIVE INTO NURTURING EMOTIONAL INTELLIGENCE AND RECOGNIZING AND MANAGING EMOTIONS EFFECTIVELY FOR IMPROVED INTERPERSONAL RELATIONSHIPS

Photo Credit: Joshua Earle https://unsplash.com/

Emotional intelligence is the compass of the heart, guiding us through the intricate terrain of human connections. By acknowledging and skillfully navigating our emotions, we cultivate the art of understanding others, fostering bonds that transcend words. In the symphony of interpersonal relationships, emotional intelligence is the conductor, orchestrating harmony through empathy and self-awareness.

—Douglas Pflug

DOI: 10.1201/9781003518099-14

MY THOUGHTS AND COMMENTARY

Emotional intelligence is the compass of the heart, guiding us through the intricate terrain of human connections. By acknowledging and skillfully navigating our emotions, we cultivate the art of understanding others, fostering bonds that transcend words. In the symphony of interpersonal relationships, emotional intelligence is the conductor, orchestrating harmony through empathy and self-awareness.

Effective employers prioritize strong people skills, fostering clear communication, conflict resolution, and employee engagement. These skills contribute to successful leadership, adaptability to change, and the ability to create a supportive work environment, ultimately promoting talent retention and legal compliance within the organization.

In my classes on facilitating "adult conversations" between employers and employees, I consistently emphasize three key points:

1. Document, document, document.
2. Always be prepared and never enter a situation unprepared.
3. Avoid having these meetings when "H.A.L.T" factors (hungry, angry, lonely, or tired) or a combination of them exist, as they can quickly sideline or derail a coaching session. With that in mind, AI can mitigate some human vulnerabilities like pride, ego, or anger from the equation, enabling more professional, efficient, and better-understood sessions for all parties involved.

Adding AI to this mix could be potentially extremely useful, but I would like to further expand this thought process and present my thoughts on two aspects of AI in the workplace when involved in the employer and employee relationships based on fears and questions, I have asked myself.

STRONG LEADERS KNOW HOW TO BALANCE IQ AND EI: WHAT HAPPENS WHEN AI COMES INTO THE EVALUATION?

Emotional intelligence (EI) and artificial intelligence (AI) serve different purposes and have distinct advantages. The main benefit of emotional intelligence, particularly in the context of human interactions, lies in its ability to understand, manage, and navigate emotions in oneself and others.

Here are some key advantages of emotional intelligence over AI:

FEARS: AI AND THE EMPLOYER/EMPLOYEE RELATIONSHIP

Integration of AI and EI: A futuristic perspective

Emotionally intelligent AI assistants

As AI advances, integrating emotional intelligence into virtual assistants may raise concerns about privacy and data security. Analyzing and responding to personal emotional cues involve potential risks.

> Pro: Virtual assistants and chatbots with emotional intelligence can significantly enhance user experience, fostering more meaningful interactions and improving overall satisfaction.
>
> Con: The development of emotionally intelligent AI may raise concerns about user privacy and data security, as it involves analyzing and responding to personal emotional cues.
>
> Leadership Strategy: Implement strict privacy measures and user consent protocols to address concerns, ensuring that emotional intelligence features prioritize user confidentiality.

Emotion recognition in human-machine interactions

The evolution of AI algorithms to recognize and respond to human emotions in real-time raises ethical concerns. Clear guidelines and regulations are necessary to prevent potential misuse of emotion recognition technology.

> Pro: Real-time emotion recognition can revolutionize fields like healthcare by enabling machines to respond effectively to patients' emotional well-being, leading to improved mental health support.
>
> Con: Ethical concerns may arise regarding the potential misuse of emotion recognition technology, emphasizing the need for clear guidelines and regulations.
>
> Leadership Strategy: Advocate for the establishment of ethical standards and collaborate with regulatory bodies to ensure responsible and transparent use of emotion recognition technology.

Adaptive learning systems

The challenge lies in ensuring that AI accurately understands and responds to diverse emotional cues in educational settings. Misinterpretations may hinder the learning process.

> Pro: Incorporating emotional intelligence in educational platforms can lead to personalized learning experiences, catering to individual students' emotional needs and enhancing overall learning outcomes.

Con: The challenge lies in ensuring that AI accurately understands and responds to diverse emotional cues, avoiding misinterpretations that may hinder the learning process.

Leadership Strategy: Continuously refine algorithms through collaboration with educators and psychologists to ensure adaptive learning systems align with diverse emotional expressions.

Sentiment analysis in business

There is a risk of misinterpretation of complex emotions, potentially leading to misunderstandings between businesses and customers.

Pro: AI tools analyzing sentiment with emotional context can provide businesses with deeper insights into customer feedback, enabling them to tailor products and services more effectively.

Con: There is a risk of misinterpretation of complex emotions, leading to potential misunderstandings between businesses and customers.

Leadership Strategy: Combine sentiment analysis with human oversight, ensuring that nuanced emotional expressions are accurately understood, and refining algorithms based on feedback.

Healthcare support

The challenge lies in maintaining a balance between AI-driven support and the human touch required in delicate healthcare situations.

Pro: AI applications assessing patients' emotional well-being can complement traditional healthcare, providing valuable support, especially in mental health applications.

Con: The challenge lies in maintaining a balance between AI-driven support and the human touch required in delicate healthcare situations.

Leadership Strategy: Design AI applications to work in tandem with healthcare professionals, emphasizing a collaborative approach that prioritizes the human connection.

Human-robot collaboration

Concerns may arise regarding the potential displacement of human workers and the need to address ethical considerations in human-robot interactions.

Pro: AI-driven robots collaborating seamlessly with humans by understanding emotions can lead to enhanced teamwork, productivity, and safety in industries like manufacturing.

Con: Concerns may arise regarding the potential displacement of human workers and the need to address ethical considerations in human-robot interactions.

Leadership Strategy: Implement training programs for human-robot collaboration, emphasizing the unique strengths each brings, and establish ethical guidelines for the integration of AI in the workforce.

Ethical AI design

Striking the right balance between innovation and ethical considerations may slow down the pace of AI development.

Pro: Prioritizing ethical AI design ensures fairness, transparency, and accountability, addressing concerns related to bias and discrimination.

Con: Striking the right balance between innovation and ethical considerations may slow down the pace of AI development.

Leadership Strategy: Foster collaboration between technologists, ethicists, and policymakers to establish a framework that promotes responsible AI development without compromising innovation.

Job displacement

The rapid integration of AI technologies in human resource management has sparked concerns about potential job displacement, potentially leading to unemployment for individuals whose responsibilities are automated.

Pro: Automation through AI can increase efficiency and productivity, allowing employees to focus on more complex and meaningful tasks.

Con: Concerns arise over potential job loss, leading to unemployment for those whose roles are automated.

Leadership Strategy: Implement retraining and upskilling programs to help employees acquire new skills that align with the evolving job landscape.

Bias and fairness

AI systems trained on historical data might perpetuate biases, potentially leading to biased hiring decisions and concerns about fairness and discrimination.

Pro: Implementing AI in the hiring process can help mitigate unconscious biases, promoting fair and data-driven decision-making that aligns with organizational values.

Con: Biases present in historical data may be perpetuated or exacerbated, leading to biased hiring decisions and concerns about fairness and discrimination.

Leadership Strategy: Implement ethical guidelines and continuous oversight to address biases in AI systems, ensuring fair and unbiased HR processes.

Privacy issues

Collection and analysis of personal data raise concerns about usage, access, and protection from unauthorized access or misuse.

Pro: Ethical data handling practices can enhance customer trust, as organizations prioritize secure data protection measures, ensuring responsible and transparent data usage.

Con: Collection and analysis of personal data raise concerns about usage, access, and protection from unauthorized access or misuse.

Leadership Strategy: Establish clear policies on data handling, prioritize secure data protection measures, and communicate transparently with employees about data usage.

Lack of human touch

Concerns arise about a potential lack of empathy and understanding as machines may struggle to interpret nuanced human emotions.

Pro: Integrating AI for efficiency can enhance overall customer service, freeing up human resources to focus on more complex, emotionally nuanced situations that require a human touch.

Con: Concerns arise about a potential lack of empathy and understanding as machines may struggle to interpret nuanced human emotions.

Leadership Strategy: Emphasize a balanced approach, integrating AI for efficiency while preserving human interactions in emotionally nuanced situations.

Transparency and accountability

Lack of transparency in AI decision-making processes, seen as "black boxes," raises concerns, especially in important HR decisions.

Pro: Transparent AI processes can build trust, as stakeholders gain insights into decision-making, fostering accountability and ensuring alignment with organizational values.

Con: Lack of transparency in AI decision-making processes, seen as "black boxes," raises concerns, especially in important HR decisions.

Leadership Strategy: Establish transparent practices, communicate how AI decisions are made, and foster accountability in HR processes.

Skills gap

Concerns about employees struggling to adapt to new skills lead to a potential skills gap and job insecurity.

Pro: Proactive training programs can empower employees, closing the skills gap and fostering a workforce capable of leveraging AI technologies for enhanced productivity.

Con: Concerns about employees struggling to adapt to new skills, leading to a potential skills gap and job insecurity.

Leadership Strategy: Implement proactive training programs and educational initiatives to empower employees for AI collaboration.

Overreliance on technology

Depending too heavily on AI for decision-making in HR could result in overreliance on technology, potentially undervaluing critical human judgment, and intuition.

Pro: Advocating for a balanced approach recognizes the complementary nature of AI and human capabilities, ensuring decisions benefit from both technological efficiency and human insight.

Con: Depending too heavily on AI for decision-making in HR could result in overreliance on technology, potentially undervaluing critical human judgment, and intuition.

Leadership Strategy: Advocate for a balanced approach, recognizing the complementary nature of AI and human capabilities in decision-making.

Ethical dilemmas

AI systems may struggle with ethical considerations in complex situations.

Pro: Prioritizing ethical AI design, involving collaboration between technologists, ethicists, and policymakers, can lead to frameworks aligning with ethical principles.

Con: AI systems may struggle with ethical considerations in complex situations.

Leadership Strategy: Prioritize ethical AI design, involving collaboration between technologists, ethicists, and policymakers to establish frameworks aligning with ethical principles.

Empathy and understanding

AI, although capable of recognizing emotional cues, lacks genuine empathy and may struggle to comprehend the nuanced and complex nature of human emotions.

Pro: Emphasizing the importance of emotional intelligence training in leadership development programs can enhance empathy and understanding in the workplace.

Con: AI, although capable of recognizing emotional cues, lacks genuine empathy and may struggle to comprehend the nuanced and complex nature of human emotions.

Leadership Strategy: Emphasize the importance of emotional intelligence training in leadership development programs to enhance empathy and understanding in the workplace.

Complex problem solving

AI, while proficient in handling specific tasks and logical problems, may struggle with the intricate complexities and nuances of human emotions in problem-solving scenarios.

Pro: Integrating emotional intelligence training into leadership development programs can enhance decision-making in complex and emotionally charged situations.

Con: AI, while proficient in handling specific tasks and logical problems, may struggle with the intricate complexities and nuances of human emotions in problem-solving scenarios.

Leadership Strategy: Integrate emotional intelligence training into leadership development programs to enhance decision-making in complex and emotionally charged situations.

Adaptability and flexibility

AI systems, designed for specific tasks, may lack the adaptability and flexibility that humans possess in adjusting to new or unforeseen circumstances.

Pro: Promoting emotional intelligence as a core competency emphasizes its role in fostering adaptability and resilience in the face of change.

Con: AI systems, designed for specific tasks, may lack the adaptability and flexibility that humans possess in adjusting to new or unforeseen circumstances.

Leadership Strategy: Promote emotional intelligence as a core competency, emphasizing its role in fostering adaptability and resilience in the face of change.

Building relationships

AI cannot form genuine emotional connections or build relationships in the same way humans do, missing the nuance of human interactions.

Pro: Integrating emotional intelligence into team-building programs enhances interpersonal connections, fostering a collaborative and emotionally intelligent work environment.

Con: AI cannot form genuine emotional connections or build relationships in the same way humans do, missing the nuance of human interactions.

Leadership Strategy: Integrate emotional intelligence training into team-building programs to strengthen interpersonal connections and collaboration.

Moral and ethical decision-making

AI systems operate based on algorithms and programming, lacking an inherent moral compass. Ethical considerations in AI decision-making are dependent on human programming and oversight.

Pro: Emphasizing the integration of emotional intelligence in ethics training enhances moral reasoning, fostering ethical decision-making in leadership.

Con: AI systems operate based on algorithms and programming, lacking an inherent moral compass. Ethical considerations in AI decision-making are dependent on human programming and oversight.

Leadership Strategy: Emphasize the integration of emotional intelligence in ethics training to enhance moral reasoning and ethical decision-making in leadership.

Enhanced interpersonal relationships

AI cannot manage emotions or form genuine connections, limiting its effectiveness in building interpersonal relationships.

Pro: Integrating emotional intelligence training into leadership development programs enhances interpersonal skills, promoting effective communication and collaboration.

Con: AI cannot manage emotions or form genuine connections, limiting its effectiveness in building interpersonal relationships.

Leadership Strategy: Integrate emotional intelligence training into leadership development programs, emphasizing its role in enhancing interpersonal skills.

Effective communication

AI cannot comprehend the emotional nuances of communication, potentially leading to misunderstandings or misinterpretations.

Pro: Incorporating emotional intelligence modules into communication training for leaders enhances their ability to understand and convey emotions, improving overall communication effectiveness.

Con: AI cannot comprehend the emotional nuances of communication, potentially leading to misunderstandings or misinterpretations.

Leadership Strategy: Incorporate emotional intelligence modules into communication training for leaders to enhance their ability to understand and convey emotions.

Conflict resolution

AI lacks the emotional understanding needed for effective conflict resolution, potentially resulting in unresolved issues.

Pro: Implementing conflict resolution workshops with a focus on emotional intelligence empowers leaders with effective conflict management skills, contributing to a harmonious work environment.

Con: AI lacks the emotional understanding needed for effective conflict resolution, potentially resulting in unresolved issues.

Leadership Strategy: Implement conflict resolution workshops with a focus on emotional intelligence to empower leaders with effective conflict management skills.

Adaptability and resilience

AI lacks the adaptability and resilience that humans possess, potentially leading to challenges in coping with change.

Pro: Integrating emotional intelligence training into change management programs enhances leaders' adaptability and resilience, facilitating smoother transitions during organizational changes.

Con: AI lacks the adaptability and resilience that humans possess, potentially leading to challenges in coping with change.

Leadership Strategy: Integrate emotional intelligence training into change management programs to enhance leaders' adaptability and resilience.

Employee engagement and motivation

AI lacks the emotional understanding required for effective employee engagement, potentially leading to a lack of motivation.

Pro: Developing leadership programs that emphasize the role of emotional intelligence contributes to creating a positive and motivating workplace, enhancing overall employee engagement.

Con: AI lacks the emotional understanding required for effective employee engagement, potentially leading to a lack of motivation.

Leadership Strategy: Develop leadership programs that emphasize the role of emotional intelligence in creating a positive and motivating workplace.

Decision-making

AI lacks inherent ethical considerations, relying on human programming and oversight for ethical decision-making.

> Pro: Integrating emotional intelligence into decision-making training enhances leaders' ability to make ethical and emotionally intelligent decisions, ensuring responsible and considerate choices.
> Con: AI lacks inherent ethical considerations, relying on human programming and oversight for ethical decision-making.
> Leadership Strategy: Integrate emotional intelligence into decision-making training to enhance leaders' ability to make ethical and emotionally intelligent decisions.

Crisis management

AI lacks the emotional understanding and stability required for effective crisis management, potentially leading to increased challenges during crises.

> Pro: Implementing crisis management training with a focus on emotional intelligence enhances leaders' ability to lead effectively during challenging times, fostering resilience and strategic decision-making.
> Con: AI lacks the emotional understanding and stability required for effective crisis management, potentially leading to increased challenges during crises.
> Leadership Strategy: Implement crisis management training with a focus on emotional intelligence to enhance leaders' ability to lead effectively during challenging times.

Innovation and collaboration

AI may struggle to facilitate effective teamwork, potentially hindering a collaborative culture.

> Pro: Integrating emotional intelligence into innovation and collaboration workshops enhances leaders' ability to create an innovative and collaborative environment, fostering a culture of creativity.
> Con: AI may struggle to facilitate effective teamwork, potentially hindering a collaborative culture.
> Leadership Strategy: Integrate emotional intelligence into innovation and collaboration workshops to enhance leaders' ability to create an innovative and collaborative environment.

Note: Responsible AI implementation and the establishment of clear policies are imperative to address concerns and create a workplace environment where AI enhances, rather than threatens, the overall employee experience.

While AI demonstrates excellence in specific tasks, recognizing the unique strengths of both emotional intelligence (EI) and AI is crucial for comprehensive and effective decision-making. The synergy between emotional intelligence and AI capabilities plays a pivotal role in achieving holistic outcomes, acknowledging the distinctive contributions each element brings to the organizational landscape.

These notes emphasize the necessity of responsible AI practices, clear policies, and the collaborative integration of emotional intelligence and AI for fostering a workplace environment that leverages the strengths of both components. In conclusion, organizations embracing these strategies and incorporating the suggested to-do list can create resilient, adaptive, and thriving workplaces.

WHAT DO HISTORY AND GENERAL RESEARCH ILLUSTRATE TO US?

Introduction: The artistry of emotional intelligence in leadership

In the dynamic evolution of leadership, the spotlight now illuminates emotional intelligence as a pivotal determinant of success.

This comprehensive exploration delves deep into the profound impact of emotional intelligence, positioning it as the guiding compass of the heart in navigating the intricacies of human connections. Leaders are not only encouraged but invited to embrace emotional intelligence as the essence that fosters a profound understanding of both them and others.

> The best leaders are those most interested in surrounding themselves with assistants and associates smarter than they are.
> —John C. Maxwell

Emotional intelligence is increasingly recognized as a critical factor in effective leadership, and its importance is likely to continue growing in 2025 and beyond. Here are several reasons why emotional intelligence is vital in leadership:

ENHANCED INTERPERSONAL RELATIONSHIPS

Leaders with high emotional intelligence can navigate and manage their own emotions effectively. This enables them to understand and connect with the emotions of others, fostering positive and meaningful interpersonal relationships. In a diverse and interconnected world, the ability to relate to people from various backgrounds and cultures is crucial.

The greatest ability in business is to get along with others and influence their actions.

—John C. Maxwell

EFFECTIVE COMMUNICATION

Emotional intelligence contributes to effective communication. Emotionally intelligent leaders can express their thoughts and ideas clearly and empathetically. They also listen actively and understand the emotions underlying the messages they receive. This is particularly important in diverse and global teams where effective communication is a cornerstone of success.

The most important thing in communication is hearing what isn't said.

—Peter Drucker

CONFLICT RESOLUTION

In any workplace, conflicts are inevitable. Leaders with emotional intelligence can navigate conflicts with finesse. They can understand the emotions driving the conflict, remain calm under pressure, and find solutions that satisfy all parties involved. This skill is crucial for supporting a positive and productive work environment.

In the middle of difficulty lies opportunity.

—Albert Einstein

ADAPTABILITY AND RESILIENCE

The business landscape is evolving rapidly, with changes in technology, markets, and working environments. Emotionally intelligent leaders are better equipped to adapt to change. They can manage their stress and anxiety, helping their teams navigate uncertainties and challenges. Resilience in the face of setbacks is a quality that is highly valued in leaders.

It is not the strongest of the species that survive, nor the most intelligent, but the one most responsive to change.

—Charles Darwin

EMPLOYEE ENGAGEMENT AND MOTIVATION

Leaders who understand the emotional needs of their team members can create a positive work environment that fosters engagement and motivation.

Recognizing and appreciating the efforts of employees, supplying constructive feedback, and creating a sense of purpose are all elements of emotional intelligence that contribute to a motivated and committed workforce.

> Your work is going to fill a large part of your life, and the only way to be truly satisfied is to do what you believe is great work.
>
> —Steve Jobs

DECISION-MAKING

Emotional intelligence plays a role in decision-making. Leaders who can weigh the emotional implications of decisions are often more adept at making well-rounded choices especially when decisions affect the lives and well-being of employees.

> In any moment of decision, the best thing you can do is the right thing, the next best thing is the wrong thing, and the worst thing you can do is nothing.
>
> —Theodore Roosevelt

CRISIS MANAGEMENT

In times of crisis, whether it be a global pandemic, economic downturn, or other challenges, emotionally intelligent leaders can supply stability. They can manage their own emotions and inspire confidence in their teams, helping the organization navigate through crises with resilience and agility.

> The only limit to our realization of tomorrow will be our doubts of today.
>
> —Franklin D. Roosevelt

INNOVATION AND COLLABORATION

Emotionally intelligent leaders can foster a culture of innovation and collaboration. They create an environment where team members feel comfortable sharing ideas, taking risks, and working together toward common goals. This collaborative approach is essential in addressing complex problems and driving innovation.

> The best way to predict the future is to create it.
>
> —Peter Drucker

In summary, emotional intelligence is crucial in leadership because it contributes to effective communication, relationship building, conflict resolution, adaptability, employee engagement, decision-making, crisis management, and fostering a culture of innovation and collaboration. As workplaces become more diverse and dynamic, the ability to navigate the emotional landscape is a key leadership skill that will continue to be highly valued.

NAVIGATING LEADERSHIP'S INTRICATE LANDSCAPE WITH EMOTIONAL INTELLIGENCE

The contemporary leadership landscape demands a nuanced comprehension of human emotions. Emotional intelligence stands as the vibrant palette from which leaders draw, crafting a masterpiece that transcends the boundaries of the professional sphere and delves into the deeply human aspects of leadership.

> Emotional intelligence is not just about individual competence; it is about the ability to connect and influence. It is the compass that guides leaders in understanding the emotional landscape, fostering collaboration, and building relationships that transcend the professional realm.
>
> —John C. Maxwell

Leaders, in this narrative, are akin to emotional architects, understanding that the foundation of a harmonious workplace rests upon the bedrock of emotional intelligence. The acknowledgment and management of emotions become the cornerstone upon which successful leadership is built.

As leaders delve into the realm of emotional intelligence, the words of Daniel Goleman become a guiding principle—"Know thyself" is not a narcissistic pursuit but a foundational principle of emotional intelligence.

Leaders are encouraged to embark on a journey of self-awareness as the first step toward understanding and mastering emotional intelligence.

EMPATHY AS THE HEARTBEAT OF LEADERSHIP: NURTURING BONDS BEYOND WORDS

Simon Sinek's insightful perspective takes center stage in exploring the second movement of the emotional intelligence symphony. This underscores the pivotal role of empathy as the heartbeat of leadership, urging leaders to recognize that emotional intelligence surpasses individual awareness—it involves genuine care and understanding for those they lead.

The essence of leadership lies in taking care of others. Empathy, as a crucial part of emotional intelligence, allows leaders to navigate the intricacies of human connections. It is the conductor that ensures the harmony of the leadership symphony, fostering bonds that transcend the limitations of words.

—Simon Sinek

Empathy becomes the bridge that connects leaders with their teams—a resonating chord that reverberates through the organizational structure, creating a culture of compassion and understanding.

As leaders embrace empathy, the enduring words of Maya Angelou resonate—"I have learned that people will forget what you said, people will forget what you did, but people will never forget how you made them feel." In the symphony of leadership, the emotional imprint left by empathetic leaders is enduring and transformative, cultivating a culture where individuals feel valued, understood, and empowered.

ORCHESTRATING HARMONY THROUGH SELF-AWARENESS: THE CONDUCTOR'S ROLE

Daniel Goleman's insightful perspective serves as the focal point for exploring the third movement in the symphony of emotional intelligence. This section contemplates the critical role of self-awareness as the conductor's baton.

Leaders are encouraged to recognize that emotional intelligence is not merely about understanding others but equally about knowing and managing their own emotions.

Emotional intelligence is a balance of knowing and managing emotions. Self-awareness is the conductor's baton that guides leaders in navigating the intricate terrain of human connections, ensuring that the harmony created is authentic, stemming from a deep understanding of one's emotional landscape.

—Daniel Goleman

Self-awareness becomes the "North Star" for leaders navigating the complex landscape of emotions—a compass guiding decisions, actions, and interactions, ensuring that the orchestrated harmony is genuine and resonates with authenticity.

As leaders orchestrate harmony through self-awareness, the words of Aristotle become a guiding principle—"Knowing yourself is the beginning of all wisdom." In the symphony of leadership, wisdom emerges from the depth of self-awareness, allowing leaders to conduct themselves with authenticity, empathy, and a profound understanding of the human experience.

CONCLUSION: THE RESONANCE OF EMOTIONAL INTELLIGENCE IN LEADERSHIP

In conclusion, the symphony of emotional intelligence stands as a masterpiece that leaders can craft in 2025 and beyond. The interconnected movements of understanding emotional intelligence, embracing empathy, and orchestrating harmony through self-awareness create a resonance that transforms leadership from a transactional role to a deeply human and enriching experience. As leaders navigate the intricate terrain of human connections with emotional intelligence as their compass, they shape a legacy of authentic leadership, fostering bonds that transcend the professional sphere.

> In the dynamic interplay between emotions and leadership, emotional intelligence emerges as the guiding force that orchestrates harmony, creating a symphony that resonates in the hearts of those who follow.
> —Unknown

This is not just a theoretical journey; it is a call to action, urging leaders to embrace and integrate these principles into their leadership philosophy.

CHAPTER "TO-DO" CHECKLIST

Intelligence Quotient Implementation

1. **Continuous Assessment:**
   Regularly assess industry trends, technological advancements, and evolving skill requirements to adapt strategies accordingly.

2. **Robust Reskilling Programs:**
   Implement comprehensive reskilling programs alongside technological integration to equip employees with evolving skill sets.

3. **Transparent Communication:**
   Communicate transparently about the responsible use of AI and data privacy policies to build trust among employees.

4. **Specialized Upskilling:**
   Collaborate with external educational institutions to offer specialized courses that align with emerging skill requirements.

5. **Feedback Mechanisms:**
   Establish regular feedback mechanisms through surveys, focus groups, or anonymous channels to identify areas for improvement.

6. Consistent Well-Being Initiatives:
Implement consistent well-being initiatives across all teams and locations to ensure a supportive work environment.

7. Personalized Leadership Development:
Provide personalized leadership development plans, mentorship programs, and continuous feedback loops to address individual differences.

8. Diversity Audits and Education Programs:
Conduct regular diversity audits, implement mentorship programs for underrepresented groups, and foster inclusivity through education and awareness programs. Address setbacks promptly and transparently.

9. Agile Talent Deployment:
Implement agile talent deployment strategies to match skillsets with evolving project needs, maximizing efficiency and adaptability.

10. Cultural Competency Training:
Provide cultural competency training to enhance awareness and understanding of diverse perspectives, fostering a more inclusive and collaborative workplace culture.

Emotional Intelligence Implementation

1. Define Emotional Intelligence:
Clearly articulate emotional intelligence as the compass of the heart, guiding leaders through the intricate terrain of human connections.

2. Emphasize Emotional Intelligence as Essence, Not Skill:
Position emotional intelligence not merely as a skill but as the essence of effective human connection, emphasizing its role in fostering collaboration and building relationships.

3. Highlight Emotional Intelligence as a Compass for Leadership:
Use John C. Maxwell's wisdom to prove emotional intelligence as the foundation for successful leadership, emphasizing its role as a compass guiding leader in understanding emotions.

4. Encourage Self-Awareness as a Foundation:
Recognize self-awareness as a foundational principle of emotional intelligence, drawing from Daniel Goleman's perspective, and encourage leaders to embark on a journey of self-awareness.

5. Embrace Empathy as Heartbeat of Leadership:
Emphasize Simon Sinek's perspective on empathy as the heartbeat of leadership, highlighting its role in genuine care and understanding of those being led.

6. **Position Empathy as Bridge Connecting Leaders and Teams:**
Illustrate empathy as the bridge connecting leaders with their teams, fostering a culture of compassion, and understanding that goes beyond the professional realm.

7. **Leave an Emotional Imprint with Empathy:**
Incorporate Maya Angelou's insight on the enduring impact of empathetic leaders, emphasizing the emotional imprint left by leaders who create a culture of value, understanding, and empowerment.

8. **Acknowledge Empathy as a Transformative Culture Catalyst:**
Reinforce the transformative impact of empathy on organizational culture, creating an environment where individuals feel valued and empowered.

9. **Recognize Self-Awareness as Conductor's Baton:**
Acknowledge self-awareness as the conductor's baton, guiding leaders in navigating the intricate terrain of human connections authentically.

10. **Conclude with Wisdom from Aristotle:**
Close this by invoking Aristotle's wisdom, emphasizing that knowing oneself is the beginning of all wisdom, and linking it to the emergence of wisdom in leadership through self-awareness.

Emotional intelligence is the compass of the heart, guiding us through the intricate terrain of human connections. By acknowledging and skillfully navigating our emotions, we cultivate the art of understanding others, fostering bonds that transcend words. In the symphony of interpersonal relationships, emotional intelligence is the conductor, orchestrating harmony through empathy and self-awareness.

—Douglas Pflug

FINAL THOUGHTS

The Heart of Leadership AI vs. EQ

Balancing the Binary: Nurturing Leadership at the Intersection of AI and EI
In the era of 2025 and beyond, leadership training delves into the delicate balance between artificial and emotional intelligence. Leaders are trained not only to leverage the power of AI but to preserve the uniquely human aspects of emotional intelligence.
Through this training, leaders gain the insights to discern when to rely on data-driven decision-making and when to tap into the empathetic qualities of emotional intelligence. The future leader navigates the intersection of AI and EI skillfully, creating a harmonious constructive collaboration between machine capabilities and human intuition.

"The Heartbeat of Leadership: AI and Emotional Intelligence in Unison"
Leadership training for 2025 is about understanding the heartbeat of leadership, where artificial intelligence and emotional intelligence work in unison. Leaders are equipped with the skills to integrate AI seamlessly into their decision-making processes while preserving the human touch that emotional intelligence provides. Training programs focus on cultivating a leadership style that acknowledges the strengths of both AI and emotional intelligence, ensuring that technology enhances rather than replaces the innate qualities that make leaders effective.

These messages underscore the importance of cultivating a nuanced understanding of the coexistence of artificial and emotional intelligence in leadership, emphasizing the need for leaders to navigate the constructive collaboration between machine-driven insights and human-centered decision-making.

CHAPTER QUOTES

1. Maya Angelou

   I have learned that people will forget what you said, people will forget what you did, but people will never forget how you made them feel.
   https://www.goodreads.com/author/quotes/3503.
   Maya_Angelou

2. Aristotle

   Knowing yourself is the beginning of all wisdom.
   https://www.goodreads.com/quotes/3690-knowing-yourself-is-the-beginning-of-all-wisdom

3. Daniel Goleman

Know thyself.

https://hbr.org/2018/01/to-improve-your-emotional-intelligence-make-a-habit-of-self-reflection

4. John C. Maxwell

The best leaders are those most interested in surrounding themselves with assistants and associates smarter than they are.

https://www.johnmaxwell.com/blog/smart-leaders-surround-themselves-with-smarter-people

5. Simon Sinek

The essence of leadership lies in taking care of others. Empathy, as a crucial part of emotional intelligence, allows leaders to navigate the intricacies of human connections. It is the conductor that ensures the harmony of the leadership symphony, fostering bonds that transcend the limitations of words.

https://www.simonsinek.com/quotes

6. Unknown

In the dynamic interplay between emotions and leadership, emotional intelligence emerges as the guiding force that orchestrates harmony, creating a symphony that resonates in the hearts of those who follow.

https://www.brainyquote.com/

Chapter 11

The Synergy of Collaboration

Photo Credit: Sydney Rae https://unsplash.com/

Encouraging Teamwork, Cooperation, and Shared Decision-Making for Collective Success

> Collaborative leadership is the compass that guides teams toward shared horizons, fostering a culture where teamwork is the engine, cooperation is the fuel, and shared decision-making is the roadmap to collective success. In the symphony of collaboration, every voice is a note, and together, we compose the melody of triumph.
>
> —Douglas Pflug

DOI: 10.1201/9781003518099-15

MY THOUGHTS AND COMMENTARY

Collaborative leadership is the compass that guides teams toward shared horizons, fostering a culture where teamwork is the engine, cooperation is the fuel, and shared decision-making is the roadmap to collective success. In the symphony of collaboration, every voice is a note, and together, we compose the melody of triumph.

As a 58-year-old man with a broad sphere of influence in various roles such as a spouse, father, son, coach, brother, uncle, police officer, strength and conditioning coach, and mentor for youth, I have encountered both failures and triumphs throughout my life, whether on an individual or collective level. The lessons extracted from these experiences have been profound.

Transitioning into my role as a leadership instructor and author, where collaborative leadership takes center stage, there are three ways I can enrich and advocate for collaborative leadership instruction, guiding us toward the future beyond 2025.

In my upcoming pursuits as a leadership instructor, I will proactively design and execute team-building exercises with a focus on fostering collaboration and nurturing camaraderie among team members.

These carefully planned activities will seek to enhance open communication, trust-building, and critical thinking skills. Through the creation of a positive and interactive environment, my goal is to empower team members to establish stronger connections and gain a profound understanding of each other's strengths and working styles.

I will actively champion inclusive decision-making processes in my role, emphasizing the importance of soliciting input from all team members and valuing their diverse perspectives and experiences. Utilizing techniques such as brainstorming sessions, roundtable discussions, and anonymous feedback channels, I will ensure that every voice is heard. This approach not only enriches the decision-making process but also fosters a sense of ownership and commitment among team members.

Furthermore, I will provide training sessions focused on effective communication strategies. These sessions will cover active listening, articulate expression of ideas, and constructive feedback. Acknowledging communication as a cornerstone of collaboration, I aim to equip team members with robust communication skills, enhancing their ability to convey thoughts, ideas, and concerns. This, in turn, will contribute to fostering a more transparent and cooperative team dynamic.

By incorporating these strategies, I aim to play a pivotal role in cultivating a collaborative leadership culture within teams, where each member actively contributes to shared success, making collaboration a guiding principle in achieving our collective goals.

WHAT DO HISTORY AND GENERAL RESEARCH ILLUSTRATE TO US?

Introduction: The rise of collaborative leadership in 2025 and beyond

In the ever-evolving landscape of leadership, the resonating call for collaborative leadership reverberates louder than ever before. This initiates a profound exploration of collaboration, positioning it as a transformative force that goes beyond merely leading a team. Collaborative leadership is akin to conducting a symphony, where each member plays a pivotal role in crafting a harmonious melody.

> Coming together is a beginning, staying together is progress, and working together is a success.
>
> —Henry Ford

COLLABORATIVE LEADERSHIP: A TRANSFORMATIVE OVERTURE

Within the progressive terrain of leadership, collaborative leaders step into the role of conductors, guiding their teams through intricate melodies of success. As we navigate the complexities of the 21st century, the principles of collaborative leadership become the compass steering us toward shared horizons, fostering a culture where every voice contributes to collective triumph.

> The strength of the team is each member. The strength of each member is the team.
>
> —Phil Jackson

THE DYNAMIC INTERPLAY OF COLLABORATIVE ELEMENTS

Exploring the core principles of collaborative leadership unveils a dynamic interplay of elements defining its essence. Each part, analogous to a musical note, contributes to the overall harmony, creating an environment where individuals not only work together but synergize toward shared goals.

Individual commitment to a group effort—that is what makes a team-work, a company work, a society work, a civilization work.

—Vince Lombardi

TEAMWORK AS THE PROPULSIVE ENGINE OF SUCCESS

Henry Ford's profound insight set the stage for exploring the first movement in the symphony of collaboration. Teamwork is not just a starting point; it is the propulsive force that propels the journey toward shared horizons. Collaborative leaders discern that the collective effort of a team surpasses the sum of individual contributions.

Never doubt that a small group of thoughtful, committed citizens can change the world; indeed, it's the only thing that ever has.

—Margaret Mead

COOPERATION AS THE CATALYST: NURTURING A CULTURE OF SUPPORT

Helen Keller's profound statement guides the exploration of the second movement in the symphony of collaboration. Cooperation is not a mere choice; it is the fuel propelling teams toward collective success. Collaborative leaders cultivate a culture where individuals support each other, and a coop-erative team achieves a far-reaching impact.

Alone, we can do so little; together, we can do so much.

—Helen Keller

SHARED DECISION-MAKING: THE ROADMAP TO COLLECTIVE EMPOWERMENT

Ken Blanchard's sagacious words become the central theme for exploring the third movement in the symphony of collaboration. Shared decision-making is not just a process; it is the roadmap empowering every voice to contribute to collective success. Collaborative leaders foster an environment where decisions are shaped by the wisdom of the team, recognizing that diverse perspectives lead to more informed choices.

The best leaders are those most interested in surrounding themselves with assistants and associates smarter than they are.

—John C. Maxwell

EVERY VOICE AS A UNIQUE NOTE: COMPOSING THE MELODY OF TRIUMPH

John Emmerling's perspective becomes the focal point for exploring the fourth movement in the symphony of collaboration. Collaborative leaders understand that Every voice is not just a sound; and the collective harmonious composition of ideas and perspectives leads to the triumph of the entire team.

Innovation distinguishes between a leader and a follower.

—Steve Jobs

CONCLUSION: A HARMONIOUS MELODY OF COLLECTIVE TRIUMPH

In conclusion, collaborative leadership serves as the compass guiding teams toward shared horizons.

The symphony of collaboration involves recognizing teamwork as the engine, cooperation as the fuel shared decision-making as the roadmap, and every voice as a note in the composition of a melodious triumph. As leaders embrace collaborative principles in 2025 and beyond, they orchestrate a harmonious symphony resonating with the success of the entire team. In the collaborative landscape of leadership, the melody of triumph is not just the achievement of individual goals but the collective success of a team that thrives in the spirit of unity and cooperation.

Alone we can do so little; together we can do so much.

—Helen Keller

CHAPTER "TO-DO" CHECKLIST

1. **Define Collaborative Leadership:**
   Clearly articulate collaborative leadership as a transformative force that guides teams toward shared horizons, emphasizing its role in fostering teamwork, cooperation, and shared decision-making.

2. **Introduce Collaborative Leaders as Conductors:**
   Position collaborative leaders as conductors in success and of leadership, guiding teams through intricate melodies toward success, and fostering a culture where every voice contributes to collective triumph.

3. **Teamwork as Propulsive Engine:**
   Explore Henry Ford's insight on teamwork as the engine propelling collective efforts toward success, emphasizing that collaborative leaders discern the surpassing value of collective team effort.

4. **Connect Teamwork to Elevated Thinking:**
   Highlight Margaret Mead's perspective on teamwork elevating thinking, encouraging leaders to recognize that collaboration brings novel perspectives and innovative solutions to complex challenges.

5. **Cooperation as Essential Fuel:**
   Emphasize Helen Keller's statement on cooperation as the fuel propelling teams toward collective success, cultivating a culture where individuals support each other, leading to far-reaching impact.

6. **Celebrate Diversity in Cooperation:**
   Integrate Vince Lombardi's insight, emphasizing that achievements result from the combined effort of everyone, highlighting how collaboration celebrates the diversity of individual talents.

7. **Shared Decision-Making as Empowerment:**
   Explore Ken Blanchard's words on shared decision-making as the roadmap empowering every voice, fostering an environment where decisions are shaped by the wisdom of the team.

8. **Highlight Diverse Perspectives in Decision-Making:**
   Emphasize the importance of diverse perspectives in decision-making, aligned with Warren Bennis' insight that leadership is the ability to translate vision into a collective reality.

9. **Every Voice as Unique Note:**
   Illustrate John Emmerling's perspective on every voice as a unique note contributing to the innovation and creativity of the collective, highlighting how collaborative leaders value diverse contributions.

10. **Enrich Collective Knowledge through Collaboration:**
    Integrate Peter Drucker's principle on collaboration allowing us to know more than we can know by ourselves, emphasizing that every voice enriches the collective knowledge and capabilities of the team.

FINAL THOUGHTS

Synergy of Collaboration

"Collaborative Leadership Mastery: Training Leaders for Collective Excellence"
In the collaborative era of 2025 and beyond, leadership training is an immersive experience in collaborative leadership mastery. Leaders are trained not only to lead individuals but to orchestrate collective excellence through collaboration. Through collaborative leadership training, leaders gain the skills to foster teamwork, encourage diverse perspectives, and create an environment where constructive collaboration enhances innovation and problem solving. Training programs empower leaders to navigate the complexities of a connected world by leveraging the collective intelligence and creativity of their teams.

"The Power of We: Training Tomorrow's Collaborative Leaders"
Leadership training for 2025 is about unlocking the power of "we." Leaders learn to transcend individual achievements and focus on collaborative success. Training programs instill the skills to build a culture of trust, open communication, and mutual respect, ensuring that constructive collaboration becomes a strategic advantage. The future leader understands that true innovation and resilience emerge from the collective efforts of a unified team.

These messages underscore the pivotal role of collaborative leadership in the future, emphasizing the need for leaders to not only value collaboration but actively cultivate an environment where the constructive collaboration of collective efforts propels organizations toward excellence.

CHAPTER QUOTES

1. Henry Ford

   Coming together is a beginning, staying together is progress, and working together is a success.

   https://en.wikiquote.org/wiki/Henry_Ford

2. Phil Jackson

   The strength of the team is each member. The strength of each member is the team.

   https://www.goodreads.com/quotes/410977-the-strength-of-the-team-is-each-individual-member-the

3. Steve Jobs

   Innovation distinguishes between a leader and a follower.

   https://www.goodreads.com/quotes/671203-innovation-distinguishes-between-a-leader-and-a-follower

4. Helen Keller

   Alone, we can do so little; together, we can do so much.

   https://www.brainyquote.com/quotes/helen-keller-164968

5. Vince Lombardi

   Individual commitment to a group effort—that is what makes a teamwork, a company work, a society work, a civilization work.

   https://www.quotemaster.org/qc/5/4/0/8/

6. John C. Maxwell

   The best leaders are those most interested in surrounding themselves with assistants and associates smarter than they are.

   https://www.goodreads.com/quotes/87664-the-best-leaders-are-those-most-interested-in-surrounding-themselves

7. Margaret Mead

   Never doubt that a small group of thoughtful, committed citizens can change the world; indeed, it's the only thing that ever has.

   https://quoteinvestigator.com/2013/12/04/small-group/

Collaborative leadership is the compass that guides teams toward shared horizons, fostering a culture where teamwork is the engine, cooperation is the fuel, and shared decision-making is the roadmap to collective success. In the symphony of collaboration, every voice is a note, and together, we compose the melody of triumph.

—Douglas Pflug

Chapter 12

Nurturing Collaborative Leadership

THE SYMPHONY OF COLLECTIVE WISDOM.

Sustainable Leadership Practices: Integrating Environmental and Social Responsibility into Leadership Approaches.

Photo Credit: Joshua Sortino https://unsplash.com/

> Sustainable leadership practices are the seeds of a flourishing future, where the soil of responsibility nourishes both the environment and society. Cultivating a garden of ethical decision-making and social consciousness, sustainable leaders sow the seeds of positive change, ensuring that every step forward is a harmonious dance with the well-being of the planet and its people.
>
> —Douglas Pflug

DOI: 10.1201/9781003518099-16

MY THOUGHTS AND COMMENTARY

"Sustainable leadership practices are the seeds of a flourishing future, where the soil of responsibility nourishes both the environment and society. Cultivating a garden of ethical decision-making and social consciousness, sustainable leaders sow the seeds of positive change, ensuring that every step forward is a harmonious dance with the well-being of the planet and its people."

As a spouse, father, and teacher, my vision for sustainable leadership practices in 2025 and beyond involves the following:

ENVIRONMENTAL EDUCATION AT HOME

In my role as a spouse and father, I am determined to weave environmental education into our family life. I will instill a robust sense of environmental responsibility in my children through daily practices such as recycling, conserving energy, and mindful consumption.

Taking the initiative, I plan to educate my family about the critical importance of sustainable living, fostering a deep understanding of how our daily choices impact the environment.

PROMOTING ECOFRIENDLY PRACTICES IN TEACHING

As a teacher, my commitment extends to incorporating ecofriendly practices into my teaching methodologies. I will integrate comprehensive lessons on sustainability and environmental consciousness across various subjects. To make these concepts tangible, I will design real-world examples and projects that emphasize responsible decision-making.

Through these initiatives, I aim to cultivate a profound sense of social consciousness and ethical leadership among my students. Additionally, within the school community, I will explore and implement strategies to minimize our environmental footprint.

COMMUNITY ENGAGEMENT FOR SUSTAINABILITY

Recognizing the interconnectedness of society, my plan involves active engagement with the local community to promote sustainable practices. Collaborating with fellow parents, educators, and community leaders, I will spearhead events, workshops, or initiatives that raise awareness about environmental issues.

By fostering a collaborative approach, we can work together to create a community that actively participates in sustainable practices. This collective commitment will contribute to the well-being of both the local environment and society at large.

In my teaching role, achieving these goals will involve designing and delivering curriculum modules that seamlessly integrate sustainability concepts. I will leverage innovative teaching methods, such as project-based learning, to make environmental education engaging and impactful for my students.

Additionally, I will collaborate with school administrators and colleagues to implement ecofriendly practices within the school infrastructure, creating a comprehensive approach to sustainable leadership in education. Through continuous communication and collaboration with the community, I aim to inspire collective action and contribute to a sustainable future.

WHAT DO HISTORY AND GENERAL RESEARCH ILLUSTRATE TO US?

The call for sustainable leadership in 2025 and beyond: Cultivating a flourishing garden of positive change

In the ever-evolving landscape of leadership, the imperative of sustainability has ascended to the forefront. This serves as an in-depth exploration into the profound essence of sustainable leadership as a transformative force for the future. Drawing parallels to gardening, sustainable leaders are envisioned as meticulous gardeners, planting seeds that germinate into a flourishing garden of positive change.

INTRODUCTION

The progressive thinking and forward-moving garden of leadership unfolds with Mahatma Gandhi's wisdom resonating as the guiding principle—the soil of responsibility serves as the foundation for positive change.

This intricately promotes thought into the soil of responsibility, emphasizing that the actions taken by leaders are reflective mirrors of their impact on both the environment and society.

In the progressive garden of leadership, Mahatma Gandhi's reflection becomes a profound truth—the soil of responsibility is not merely the foundation for positive change; it is a reflective mirror that reveals the values and actions of sustainable leaders. Leaders are impelled to recognize the interconnectedness of their decisions with the well-being of the planet and its people.

> The best way to find yourself is to lose yourself in the service of others.
>
> —Mahatma Gandhi

RESPONSIBILITY AS FERTILE SOIL

This fertile soil of responsibility is where sustainable leaders plant the seeds of positive change, fostering a culture of conscious decision-making. It calls for leaders to make decisions with an acute awareness of their ripple effect on the broader ecosystem.

As leaders cultivate the soil of responsibility, the timeless words of Wendell Berry resonate—the earth is what we all have in common. In the garden of leadership, this common ground symbolizes the shared responsibility of sustainable leaders to nurture both the environment and society, leaving a legacy of positive impact.

> The earth does not belong to us: we belong to the earth.
>
> —Wendell Berry

ETHICAL DECISION-MAKING: SEEDS FOR A FLOURISHING FUTURE

The Chinese proverb takes center stage in the second movement of sustainable leadership, emphasizing the profound significance of ethical decision-making as the seeds that leaders plant for a flourishing future. In the progressive garden of leadership, ethical decision-making is not a matter of hindsight; it is a deliberate act of planting seeds in the present for a bountiful harvest in the future.

This underscores ethical decision-making as the intentional act of planting—the conscious choice to sow seeds that will grow into a canopy of positive outcomes. Sustainable leaders recognize that the best time for ethical decision-making is now, with each decision being a seed for the future.

> He who plants a tree plants a hope.
>
> —Chinese proverb

LEADERS AS EXPERT GARDENERS

The words of John C. Maxwell serve as a guiding light, resonating within the garden of progressive leadership—a leader knows the way, goes the way, and shows the way. Ethical leaders, akin to expert gardeners, pave the way for a flourishing future. They prove an unwavering commitment to principles that transcend short-term gains, ensuring that the seeds they plant today bear fruits of success and positive change.

A leader knows the way, goes the way, and shows the way.

—John C. Maxwell

CULTIVATING SOCIAL CONSCIOUSNESS: NOURISHING THE ROOTS OF CHANGE

Franklin D. Roosevelt's perspective takes center stage in the third movement of sustainable leadership. This promotes thought into the paramount importance of cultivating social consciousness as the nourishment for the roots of positive change. In the progressive garden of leadership, Roosevelt's words resonate—social consciousness is the vital nourishment that sustains the roots of positive change. Sustainable leaders are urged to overcome doubts and embrace a future where every step forward is a harmonious dance with societal well-being.

Cultivating social consciousness becomes analogous to tending to the roots of the garden. Sustainable leaders recognize the interconnectedness of their actions with the broader societal ecosystem, understanding that positive change requires nurturing the very essence of collective well-being.

The only limit to our realization of tomorrow will be our doubts of today.

—Franklin D. Roosevelt

MOTHER TERESA'S WISDOM

As leaders cultivate social consciousness, the profound words of Mother Teresa become a guiding principle—the impact of individual actions, small, collectively contribute to waves of positive change. In the garden of leadership, sustainable leaders understand the collective influence of these individual drops, collectively creating waves that transform the landscape of society.

I alone cannot change the world, but I can cast a stone across the waters to create many ripples.

—Mother Teresa

CONCLUSION: HARVESTING THE FRUITS OF SUSTAINABLE LEADERSHIP

In conclusion, sustainable leadership practices stand as the seeds that leaders sow today for a flourishing future. The interconnected movements of nurturing the soil of responsibility, planting seeds through ethical decision-making, and cultivating social consciousness create a symphony that resonates with the well-being of both the planet and its people.

As leaders embrace sustainability, they embark on a journey of responsibility, ethics, and social consciousness, ensuring that every step forward is a harmonious dance with the future. In the garden of sustainable leadership, the fruits harvested are not just success but a legacy of positive change that endures and enriches the world.

Furthermore, sustainable leadership extends beyond environmental stewardship and encompasses a holistic approach to long-term viability. It involves fostering resilience, promoting diversity and inclusion, and prioritizing the well-being of stakeholders at all levels. By adopting sustainable practices, leaders can create organizations that thrive in the face of challenges, contribute positively to society, and leave a lasting legacy for generations to come.

> The best time to plant a tree was 20 years ago. The second-best time is now.
>
> —Chinese proverb

As leaders continue to sow these seeds in 2025 and beyond, they contribute to a garden where the environment thrives, and society flourishes—a testament to the enduring impact of sustainable leadership.

CULTIVATING A FLOURISHING GARDEN: THE COMPREHENSIVE BOOK TO SUSTAINABLE LEADERSHIP IN 2025 AND BEYOND

In this comprehensive book, we embark on a profound exploration of sustainable leadership, delving into its multifaceted dimensions and offering actionable insights for leaders committed to fostering positive change. As we journey through the realms of responsibility, ethical decision-making, and social consciousness, we unveil the intricate nuances that elevate sustainable leadership beyond mere necessity, positioning it as a potent catalyst for shaping a brighter future.

THE ESSENCE OF RESPONSIBILITY IN SUSTAINABLE LEADERSHIP

At the core of sustainable leadership lies the essence of responsibility. Mahatma Gandhi's wisdom echoed throughout history and emphasizes that this responsibility is not just a foundational soil but a mirror reflecting the values and actions of leaders. In our exploration, we will scrutinize the soil of responsibility, understanding how leaders can cultivate it to yield a garden of positive change.

Leaders are beckoned to recognize the interconnectedness of their decisions with the broader ecosystem. This recognition becomes the first step in cultivating the fertile soil of responsibility. We will examine real-world examples of leaders who have successfully embraced this responsibility, making decisions with a keen awareness of their environmental and societal impact.

> The best way to predict the future is to create it.
>
> —Peter Drucker

The words of Wendell Berry function as a beacon, reminding us that the earth is what we all have in common. Through case studies and practical strategies, we will illuminate how leaders, as stewards of the earth, can nurture this common ground, ensuring that the legacy they leave is one of positive impact.

SEEDS OF ETHICAL DECISION-MAKING: SOWING TODAY FOR A FLOURISHING TOMORROW

Building on the foundation of responsibility, ethical decision-making emerges as the seeds that leaders plant for a flourishing future. We will dissect the Chinese proverb's wisdom, exploring how ethical decisions are not hindsight reflections but intentional acts of planting seeds in the present.

Ethical decision-making becomes a deliberate choice—a conscious effort to sow seeds that will blossom into a canopy of positive outcomes. Drawing parallels between leadership and expert gardening, we will uncover the characteristics of ethical leaders who, like skilled gardeners, know the way, go the way, and show the way.

> Ethics is knowing the difference between what you have a right to do and what is right to do.
>
> —Potter Stewart

John C. Maxwell's profound words will book us through this exploration, underscoring that a leader's role is to pave the way for a flourishing future. We will examine case studies of leaders who have successfully integrated ethical decision-making into their leadership styles, reaping long-term rewards.

CULTIVATING SOCIAL CONSCIOUSNESS: NOURISHING THE ROOTS OF POSITIVE CHANGE

Moving to the third movement, we will shine a spotlight on the paramount importance of cultivating social consciousness as the nourishment for the roots of positive change. Franklin D. Roosevelt's perspective becomes our compass, urging us to overcome doubts and embrace a future where every step forward is a harmonious dance with societal well-being.

Cultivating social consciousness becomes analogous to tending to the roots of the garden. In this section, we will explore how sustainable leaders recognize the interconnectedness of their actions with the broader societal ecosystem. Practical strategies and case studies will illustrate how leaders can contribute to positive change by nurturing the very essence of collective well-being.

> Alone, we can do so little; together, we can do so much.
> —Helen Keller

Mother Teresa's wisdom will serve as a guiding principle, reminding us that the impact of individual actions, though seemingly small, collectively contributes to waves of positive change. Through inspiring stories and actionable insights, we will delve into the collective influence of these individual drops, collectively creating waves that transform the landscape of society.

CONCLUSION: A SYMPHONY OF SUSTAINABLE LEADERSHIP

In the concluding chapters of our comprehensive book, we will weave together the threads of responsibility, ethical decision-making, and social consciousness. The symphony of sustainable leadership will resonate with the well-being of both the planet and its people, presenting leaders with a roadmap for fostering enduring positive change.

The fruits harvested in the garden of sustainable leadership are not merely success but a legacy that endures and enriches the world. As leaders continue to sow these seeds in 2025 and beyond, they contribute to a garden where the environment thrives, and society flourishes—a testament to the enduring impact of sustainable leadership.

> The best way to find yourself is to lose yourself in the service of others.
> —Mahatma Gandhi

CHAPTER "TO-DO" CHECKLIST

1. **Define Sustainable Leadership:**
   Clearly articulate sustainable leadership as a transformative force for the future, drawing parallels to gardening and emphasizing the responsibility to sow seeds for positive change.

2. **Emphasize Responsibility as Soil Foundation:**
   Position responsibility as the foundation for positive change, echoing Mahatma Gandhi's reflection that the soil of responsibility mirrors the values and actions of sustainable leaders.

3. **Connect Actions to Interconnected Impact:**
   Illustrate the interconnectedness of leaders' actions with the well-being of the planet and its people, emphasizing the reflection in the soil of responsibility.

4. **Incorporate Wendell Berry's Insight:**
   Use Wendell Berry's insight to reinforce the common ground shared by sustainable leaders—the earth—and highlight the responsibility to nurture the environment and society.

5. **Highlight Ethical Decision-Making as Seeds:**
   Position ethical decision-making as seeds for a flourishing future, drawing from the Chinese proverb's wisdom that the best time to plant a tree was 20 years ago, and the second-best time is now.

6. **Emphasize Present and Future Impact:**
   Reinforce the notion that ethical decision-making is about the present and the future, echoing the Chinese proverb, and encouraging leaders to plant seeds for positive change now.

7. **Use John C. Maxwell's Leadership Principle:**
   Incorporate John C. Maxwell's leadership principle, emphasizing that ethical leaders know the way, go the way, and show the way, highlighting the commitment to principles that transcend short-term gains.

8. **Cultivate Social Consciousness as Root Nourishment:**
   Emphasize cultivating social consciousness as nourishment for the roots of positive change, drawing from Franklin D. Roosevelt's perspective on overcoming doubts for a harmonious dance with societal well-being.

9. **Acknowledge Collective Impact of Individual Actions:**
   Incorporate Mother Teresa's principle, highlighting those individual actions, though seemingly small, collectively contribute to waves of positive change, reinforcing the collective impact of sustainable leaders.

10. **Conclude with Fruits of Sustainable Leadership:**
    Close this by emphasizing that sustainable leadership practices yield fruits of success and a legacy of positive change, contributing to a flourishing future where the environment thrives, and society is enriched.

Sustainable leadership practices are the seeds of a flourishing future, where the soil of responsibility nourishes both the environment and society. Cultivating a garden of ethical decision-making and social consciousness, sustainable leaders sow the seeds of positive change, ensuring that every step forward is a harmonious dance with the well-being of the planet and its people.

—Douglas Pflug

FINAL THOUGHTS

Nurturing Collaborative Leadership:
"Cultivating Collaborative Leadership: Training Tomorrow's Team Orchestras"
In the collaborative landscape of 2025 and beyond, leadership training is a transformative journey in cultivating collaborative leadership. Leaders are trained not only to lead teams but to orchestrate them like conductors guiding symphonies. Through collaborative leadership training, leaders gain the skills to foster a culture of shared purpose, trust, and open communication. Training programs empower leaders to navigate complexities by leveraging the diverse strengths of their teams, ensuring that collaboration becomes the cornerstone of organizational success.

"Leading Together: Nurturing Collaborative Leadership in the Digital Age"
Leadership training for 2025 is about leading together in the digital age. Leaders learn to harness the power of technology to enhance collaboration while preserving the human touch. Training programs focus on equipping leaders with the skills to cultivate teamwork, encourage idea-sharing, and create a collaborative environment where innovation flourishes. The future leader understands that collaborative leadership is not just a skill but a strategic imperative for sustainable success.

These messages underscore the importance of nurturing collaborative leadership in the future, emphasizing the need for leaders to not only facilitate collaboration but actively cultivate an environment where teams thrive through shared purpose, open communication, and collective innovation.

CHAPTER QUOTES

1. **Wendell Berry**

   The earth does not belong to us: we belong to the earth.
   https://www.goodreads.com/quotes/198864-the-earth-does-not-belong-to-us-we-belong-to

2. **Chinese Proverb**

   He who plants a tree plants a hope.
   https://www.goodreads.com/quotes/155351-he-who-plants-a-tree-plants-a-hope

3. **Peter Drucker**

   The best way to predict the future is to create it.
   https://www.goodreads.com/quotes/157971-the-best-way-to-predict-the-future-is-to-create

4. **Mahatma Gandhi**

   The best way to find yourself is to lose yourself in the service of others.
   https://www.brainyquote.com/quotes/mahatma_gandhi_150177

5. **Helen Keller**

   Alone, we can do so little; together, we can do so much.
   https://www.brainyquote.com/quotes/helen-keller-164968

6. **John C. Maxwell**

   A leader knows the way, goes the way, and shows the way.
   https://www.goodreads.com/quotes/6725460-a-leader-is-one-who-knows-the-way-goes-the

7. **Mother Teresa**

   I alone cannot change the world, but I can cast a stone across the waters to create many ripples.
   https://www.goodreads.com/quotes/567715-i-alone-cannot-change-the-world-but-i-can-cast

8. **Franklin D. Roosevelt**

The only limit to our realization of tomorrow will be our doubts of today.
https://www.brainyquote.com/quotes/franklin-d-roosevelt-403152

9. **Potter Stewart**

Ethics is knowing the difference between what you have a right to do and what is right to do.
https://www.brainyquote.com/quotes/potter_stewart_119569

Conclusion

A Call to Action

Photo Source: Shane Rounce https://unsplash.com/@shanerounce

All my life I've consistently tried to lead with a service heart, embracing both pain and joy in my relentless pursuit of bettering others. Witnessing someone else rise from the background in the end isn't just a reward; it's the embodiment of a meaningful legacy.

—D. Pflug

DOI: 10.1201/9781003518099-17

WILL YOU ANSWER THE CALL TO ACTION?

> Help others and give something back. I guarantee you will discover that while public service improves the lives and the world around you, its greatest reward is the enrichment and new meaning it will bring your own life.
>
> —Arnold Schwarzenegger

Thank you for embarking on this transformative journey of personal leadership, aligning progressive thoughts to craft comprehensive personal, professional, and positional plans, and setting the stage to #RiseUpAndExcel beyond 2025. As we conclude our shared exploration of forward-thinking leadership principles, let's delve deeper into the profound impact that service, charity, and philanthropy can wield on individuals and communities.

Just as I presented in my previous book, *Finding Your Granite*, with its four cornerstones of personal leadership, I challenge you once again: "Make a stranger smile, or better yet, mentor a young person." The potential unleashed through these small acts of kindness is immeasurable.

Always remember, you possess the opportunity, skills, desire, and responsibility to uplift those around you, leaving them better than before they crossed paths with you.

Service to others: A foundation for leadership excellence

> The best way to find yourself is to lose yourself in the service of others.
> —Mahatma Gandhi

True leadership transcends self-interest, finding its roots in service to others. Consider service as a foundational pillar of your leadership philosophy.

Embrace the power of selfless contribution, recognizing that by uplifting those around you, you elevate not just yourself but also the collective spirit of your community. Uncover innovative ways to weave acts of service into your daily leadership practice, fostering a culture of collaboration and shared success.

Charity as a guiding light: Illuminating paths of compassion

> No one has ever become poor by giving.
> —Anne Frank

Charity serves as a guiding light, illuminating the path to a more compassionate world. Explore the myriad ways in which acts of charity, both big and small, can have a profound impact on individuals and communities.

Delve into the intricacies of charitable giving, understanding that each act of kindness contributes to a tapestry of positive change. Cultivate a mindset where charity becomes an integral part of your leadership journey, fostering a legacy of empathy and generosity.

The transformative impact of philanthropy: Beyond individual contributions

> Philanthropy is not about money. It's about using whatever resources you have at your fingertips and applying them to improving the world.
>
> —Melinda Gates

Philanthropy is the catalyst for systemic change. Dive deeper into the transformative power of philanthropy and explore how your resources—whether time, skills, or financial means—can be strategically deployed to address societal challenges.

Reflect on the responsibility that comes with privilege and leverage it to effect positive, lasting change. Develop a philanthropic strategy that aligns with your values and vision, leaving an indelible mark on the world through purposeful and impactful giving.

Building bridges of empathy: Strengthening leadership connections

> Leadership is not about being in charge. It's about taking care of those in your charge.
>
> —Simon Sinek

In a world often marked by division, cultivate empathy as a central tenet of your leadership approach.

Examine ways to understand the diverse perspectives and needs of those you lead. Building bridges of empathy fosters a sense of unity and inclusivity, creating an environment where collective growth and success can flourish. Dive into the nuances of empathetic leadership, recognizing its role in creating cohesive and resilient teams that thrive in an atmosphere of mutual understanding.

It is not what you do, but rather the fact that you are doing it.

Holistic spirituality: Doing the right thing because it's the right thing to do

> Ethical leadership is not about being religious; it's about doing the right thing because it's the right thing to do. It's a recognition of our shared humanity and the interconnectedness of all life.
>
> —Douglas Pflug

Beyond the realms of traditional leadership principles lies the profound realm of holistic spirituality. In this space, the focus shifts towards doing the right thing simply because it aligns with a universal sense of ethical responsibility. Holistic spirituality invites you to transcend religious boundaries and connect with a deeper understanding of your role in the intricate tapestry of existence.

Engage in acts of kindness, service, and generosity not driven by external doctrines but by an innate recognition of the interconnectedness of all life. Embrace a comprehensive approach that encompasses the well-being of individuals, communities, and the environment. Strive for a leadership that operates from a place of authenticity, integrity, and a commitment to the greater good.

In cultivating holistic spirituality, the emphasis is on cultivating a genuine desire to contribute positively to the world, fostering a sense of responsibility for the well-being of all living beings and the planet. By doing the right thing because it's the right thing to do, you elevate your leadership to a level that transcends personal gain, leaving a lasting legacy of compassion and ethical influence.

As you continue your journey of personal leadership, may the integration of holistic spirituality guide your actions, decisions, and interactions, contributing to a world where leadership is not only impactful but also deeply rooted in a profound sense of shared humanity.

A pledge for sustainable leadership: Charting your ongoing impact

> The greatest leader is not necessarily the one who does the greatest things. He is the one that gets the people to do the greatest things.
> —Ronald Reagan

As you close this chapter, please take a moment for a comprehensive reflection on your commitment to sustainable leadership. Pledge to continuously refine your leadership skills, nurture a culture of inclusivity, and actively contribute to the betterment of society.

Recognize that your leadership journey is an ongoing narrative, one that unfolds with every decision and action. Let it be a story of positive impact, shared prosperity, and a legacy that transcends time. You were all born with light; make it stronger and help brighten the lives of others

In the spirit of service, charity, and philanthropy, let us collectively strive for a world where leadership is defined by its capacity to uplift, inspire, and create enduring positive change.

Thank you for being an integral part of this transformative exploration. May unwavering compassion, resilience, and a steadfast commitment mark your leadership journey to making a lasting difference.

I can, I must, I will!!!

2025 personal mantra

Leading with my best self
Model the behaviour I seek of others
Always creating an environment where others can succeed
Take care of yourself to enable me to care for others.

With heartfelt gratitude,
Douglas Pflug

Throughout our journey, we've upheld the ethos of servant leadership, navigating through trials and triumphs with unwavering resolve to uplift those around us. Yet, our mission is far from complete. It's time to transcend our current paradigms, to evolve the way we guide ourselves, our businesses, our teams, and our organizations.

Let us courageously embrace emerging trends, anticipate future challenges, and harness the collective power within us to #RiseUpAndExcel.

For in the ascent of each individual from obscurity lies the true testament of our legacy, a legacy defined not by personal accolades, but by the transformative impact we impart on others.

—Douglas Pflug

The seven sacred teachings

Joffre and I met in early grade school, and upon reflection, we had no idea of the similarity we shared at the time. We were only young boys and did not have the knowledge, strength, or power to enact change.

Our story was quite simple and took place around 1973–1975 during "story time" at school. At that time, we barely knew each other but often found ourselves sitting alone on the bare floor and not on the "story time carpet" with the other students while the teacher read to us.

When I retired from policing, Joffre came to my party with a bottle of McClellan. After we caught up and spoke, he drove home to retrieve "The Hunter" because he felt that we both needed each other.

Upon his return, he further told me "That sculpture has its own spirit, and it will give you the medicine you need." It was an incredible honor to have Joffre attend the function after all these years and present me with an incredible piece of art and story, entitled "The Hunter," that he had created. Or, as he advised, the clay moved his hands to create this amazing masterpiece.

As we chatted, we reflected back on the days when we met and spoke of the story time in class. What we both didn't realize is that our separation from the class was a targeted act. I shared that the teacher made fun of where I lived, and Joffre shared the humiliating news that the teacher snatched his prized "show and tell" object, a partridge claw and feathers and threw them in the trash bin, then said, "You are nothing but a disgusting dirty little savage." Not being able to sit on the plush reading carpet was humiliating indeed. He further stated, "I now own that I am untamed and know that being a savage is a compliment."

I remember the pain I saw in his eyes from an experience 40 years ago, but it stung, and I once again vowed to speak up for those who suffer ignorance in all forms.

Joffre then spoke of The Seven Sacred Teachings originating from the Seven Grandfather Teachings of the Anishinaabe people and adopted by many (but not all) First Nations, Métis, and Inuit Peoples. The teachings focus on the relationships we have with all of creation and offer ways on how people should treat others. The seven teachings include love, respect, honesty, courage/bravery, truth, wisdom, and humility, and each teaching is represented by an animal. Each animal helps teach us how we can live our lives respecting animals, people, and the environment—every living thing. It should be noted that these teachings may differ slightly between groups or cultures.

What incredible knowledge and reflection he bestowed on that day, a gift and knowledge to be the change we need in this world.

This book speaks directly to forward-thinking leaders, urging them to not only absorb the wisdom of the past but also to embrace the profound significance of the seven timeless teachings: love, respect, honesty, courage/bravery, truth, wisdom, and humility. Like the phoenix rising from the ashes, these teachings symbolize the rebirth of leadership values and principles that have endured the test of time, transcending generations.

As leaders delve into the pages of this book, they are called upon to embody these teachings in their actions and decisions, serving as beacons of integrity, compassion, and vision. By internalizing these values, leaders can cultivate environments of trust, foster authentic connections, and inspire others to strive for excellence.

Furthermore, this book serves as a reminder that progressive leadership is not a solitary journey but a collective endeavor. It emphasizes the importance of collaboration, partnership, and inclusivity in driving meaningful change. Leaders are encouraged to reach out, build bridges, and forge alliances with diverse stakeholders, recognizing that true progress is achieved through unity and cooperation.

Moreover, the book underscores the imperative of innovation and adaptability in navigating the complexities of today's world. It challenges leaders to embrace creativity, embrace change, and embrace change as opportunities for growth and transformation. By embracing a mindset of continuous learning and innovation, leaders can stay ahead of the curve, anticipate challenges, and seize opportunities for positive change.

Thanks, my friend.

"The Hunter"

"The Hunter" has a vision and a gaze that looks through this world to next. His ears are perked, and his hearing reaches out miles and miles through the bush and beyond. He also hears in the spirit world. He sits calm, his heart slowed, and a lone Raven will gnaw with his raspy voice, a red squirrel will chatter, and the chickadees will swirl around, often sitting on his bow as a beaver slips into the water and a loon sings way off over the North Channel. Winds blow through the birch, cedars, maples, and oak to create the cacophony along with the animals. It all sharpens to one tone. His nostrils are flared taking in the smell of earth, moss, and wet leaves at his feet. He can smell winter far off on the northern wind and smell the North Channel along with the cedars where he has perched. His head is slightly cocked to one side, he is one with the bush, one with the universe. He knows that he will meet his deer today, they made a pact in a vision. He asked the mother earth to receive both their steps on their path today. He thanks the buck and sends him to the spirit world. This is "The Hunter" he watches over you. Happy Retirement Brother and May your footsteps always be received and steadied on your path. I am not surprised that his gaze has captivated you. It is a common comment. The fact that you like it, means the world to me. I love you too my friend. Glad our paths cross.

Artist: Joffre O Perreault III

Joffre is Odawa and a member of the Sheshegwaning First Nations Manitoulin Island.

Odawa is part of the Anishinaabe Nation like Ojibwa and Potawanami.

CHAPTER QUOTES

1. **Anne Frank**

   No one has ever become poor by giving.
   Quote by Anne Frank: "No one has ever become poor by giving." (goodreads.com)

2. **Melinda Gates**

   Philanthropy is not about money. It's about using whatever resources you have at your fingertips and applying them to improving the world.
   This I Believe: Being Philanthropic | by Mary Alice Lasswell | GMWP: Greater Madison Writing Project | Medium

3. **Mahatma Gandhi**

   The best way to find yourself is to lose yourself in the service of others.

Define the following Mahatma Gandhi quote: "The best way to find yourself is to lose yourself in the service of others."

—eNotes.com

4. Ronald Reagan

The greatest leader is not necessarily the one who does the greatest things. He is the one that gets the people to do the greatest things.

The greatest leader is not necessarily the one who does the greatest things. He is the one that gets the people to do the greatest things. | Contemporary Quotations (american.edu)

5. Arnold Schwarzenegger

Help others and give something back. I guarantee you will discover that while public service improves the lives and the world around you, its greatest reward is the enrichment and new meaning it will bring your own life.

Help others and give something back. I guarantee you will discover that while public service improves the lives and the world around you, its greatest reward is the enrichment and new meaning it will bring to your own life. (elevatesociety.com)

6. Simon Sinek

Leadership is not about being in charge. It's about taking care of those in your charge.

Leadership is not about being in charge. Leadership is about taking care of those in your charge.

—AskTheRightQuestion

RESEARCH RESOURCES

Photo credit: Aleks Dorohovich https://unsplash.com/@doctype

1. Harvard Business Review—Leadership
   https://hbr.org/topic/leadership
2. Forbes—Leadership
   https://www.forbes.com/leadership
3. CCL—Center for Creative Leadership
   https://www.ccl.org/
4. TED Talks on Leadership
   https://www.ted.com/topics/leadership
5. Mind Tools—Leadership Styles
   https://www.mindtools.com/pages/article/newLDR_84.htm
6. Leadership Freak Blog
   https://leadershipfreak.blog/
7. Very Well Mind—Different Leadership Styles
   https://www.verywellmind.com/types-of-leadership-styles-5176000
8. Gallup—Leadership
   https://www.gallup.com/workplace/285674/how-to-be-a-good-leader.aspx
9. The Leadership Challenge
   https://www.leadershipchallenge.com/
10. Jim Collins—Level 5 Leadership
    https://www.jimcollins.com/concepts/level-5-leadership.html

11. Psychology Today—Leadership Styles
https://www.psychologytoday.com/us/basics/leadership
12. Harvard Business Review—The Art of Leadership
https://hbr.org/2017/11/the-art-of-leadership
13. MIT Sloan Management Review—Artificial Intelligence
https://sloanreview.mit.edu/topic/artificial-intelligence/
14. Harvard Business Review—AI in the Workplace
https://hbr.org/insight-center/artificial-intelligence
15. McKinsey—AI and the Future of Work
https://www.mckinsey.com/featured-insights/artificial-intelligence
16. World Economic Forum—The Future of Jobs Report
http://www3.weforum.org/docs/WEF_Future_of_Jobs_2018.pdf
17. Forrester—AI-Powered Customer Experience
https://go.forrester.com/research/forrester-predictions-2020/
18. Harvard Business Review—AI-Enhanced Decision Making
https://hbr.org/2021/08/how-ai-is-improving-decision-making
19. Ethical Considerations in AI—Stanford University
https://ethicsinaction.ieee.org/
20. AI and Ethics—Stanford Encyclopedia of Philosophy
https://plato.stanford.edu/entries/ethics-ai/
21. The Future of Life Institute —AI Ethics
https://futureoflife.org/ai-ethics/
22. AI Literacy—Coursera
https://www.coursera.org/learn/ai-for-everyone
23. AI4ALL—Resources for AI Education
https://ai4all.org/resources/
24. Creativity and Artificial Intelligence—Forbes
https://www.forbes.com/sites/forbestechcouncil/2018/12/07/ai-creativity-the-key-to-success-in-the-digital-age/?sh=7d12ed625ea3
25. Futurism—Emerging Technologies
https://futurism.com/tags/emerging-technology
26. Communication Skills - LinkedIn Learning
https://www.linkedin.com/learning/topics/communication-skills
27. Communication in the Workplace—Skills You Need
https://www.skillsyouneed.com/interpersonal-skills/workplace-communication.html
28. The Evolution of Communication—Medium
https://medium.com/@adithyabsk/the-evolution-of-communication-47a8c1933337
29. Communication Technology Trends—Deloitte
https://www2.deloitte.com/us/en/insights/industry/technology/tech-trends/2022/communications-technology.html
30. Communication Styles—Very well Mind
https://www.verywellmind.com/types-of-communication-2795427

31. Leadership Communication—Harvard Business Review
    https://hbr.org/2018/12/the-key-to-better-communication
32. Technology and Leadership—Training Industry
    https://trainingindustry.com/articles/leadership/how-does-technology-affect-leadership-today/
33. The Role of Technology in Communication—Business News Daily
    https://www.businessnewsdaily.com/6302-technology-in-business-communication.html
34. Open Communication in the Workplace—SHRM
    https://www.shrm.org/resourcesandtools/hr-topics/employee-relations/pages/opencommunication.aspx
35. The Importance of Open Communication—Indeed Career Guide
    https://www.indeed.com/career-advice/career-development/open-communication
36. Leadership Communication Styles—Psychology Today
    https://www.psychologytoday.com/us/blog/the-leadership-advantage/201307/understanding-leadership-styles
37. Effective Communication Strategies—Forbes
    https://www.forbes.com/sites/forbescoachescouncil/2017/12/13/14-effective-communication-strategies-to-use-in-the-workplace/?sh=38a62e1226cc
38. Emotional Intelligence—Daniel Goleman
    https://www.danielgoleman.info/topics/emotional-intelligence/
39. Emotional Intelligence in Leadership—MindTools
    https://www.mindtools.com/pages/article/newLDR_45.htm
40. Continuous Learning—LinkedIn Learning
    https://www.linkedin.com/learning/topics/continuous-learning
41. Adaptive Leadership—Harvard Business Review
    https://hbr.org/2009/11/adaptability-the-new-competitive-advantage

FINDING YOUR GRANITE: MY FOUR CORNERSTONES OF PERSONAL LEADERSHIP

Introduction

In 2022, we embarked on a heartfelt journey with the launch of *Finding Your Granite: Four Cornerstones of Personal Leadership*. Our mission was twofold: to offer readers invaluable insights into personal leadership and to extend a helping hand to those who have served our communities selflessly. Through this endeavor, we pledged to donate 100% of our profits to support veterans and everyday heroes, specifically by providing support dogs to frontline workers coping with PTSD through the wonderful charity Veterans and Everyday Heroes (www.V-eh.ca).

We're thrilled to share that our efforts have borne fruit, allowing us to contribute over $7,000.00 CDN to this noble cause. And this is just the beginning. Each year, we're committed to continuing this support, ensuring that more individuals receive the assistance they require.

This project holds profound significance for our author, Douglas Pflug, who himself has grappled with PTSD through his 36 years in law enforcement. Having experienced firsthand the transformative power of a service dog, Douglas understands the immense impact such companions can have on the lives of those struggling with PTSD. It's this personal connection that inspired him to initiate this project, recognizing the financial barriers that may prevent frontline workers from accessing the support they deserve.

If you're interested in owning your own personalized copy of *Finding Your Granite*, we invite you to visit www.riseupandexcel.ca. Additionally, the book is available for purchase on Amazon and the Taylor Francis website.

Finding Your Granite isn't just a book; it's a beacon of hope and empowerment. Through its pages, readers embark on a journey of self-discovery and leadership, all while contributing to a cause that uplifts our everyday heroes. Join us in spreading kindness and making a difference, one page at a time.

Abstract

In *Finding Your Granite*, Executive Leadership Coach and Mentor Douglas Pflug walks you through some of the life experiences, lessons, and key takeways from his years as a dual sport university athlete, 28 years as a police officer, 30 years as an elite strength and conditioning coach, mentor, and leader.

Douglas accomplishes this through four very dynamic, energetic, and heartfelt sections entitled: "The Struggle," "Dash Leadership," "Four Cornerstones of Personal Leadership," and "Rise Up and Excel." The Author's mentoring and protégé process and implementation of #RiseUpAndExcel and #StrongerFasterFitter methodologies assist people in discovering "who they were, who they are and whom they want to be" moving forward in this post-COVID-19 world.

This book was written through the eyes of an "everyday guy" and designed to educate, entertain, and inspire front line 911 emergency workers to seek and achieve their potential. Additionally, this book will also be an essential resource for individuals and business leaders who wish to stay ahead of the evolving leadership trends of strategic thinking, inspiration and motivation, strong interpersonal skills, vision, decisiveness, and passion.

Finding Your Granite excerpt

Doctors told Paul and Joan Pflug to say goodbye to their newborn son as he underwent life-saving surgery in 1966 at six days old.

Although the first surgery was considered a success, he again fell ill at three years old. He was hospitalized so the doctors could start treatment for what they believed to be childhood leukemia.

One can only imagine the stress this young couple in their early twenties faced while dealing with their sick little boy. This was the 1960s, so many medical advancements that are known today had yet to be discovered. It is difficult to imagine the paralyzing fear and devastation that these two incredibly young parents had experienced with the suffering and possible death of their baby.

Miraculously Doug survived. Since that time, he has displayed incredible physical, emotional, and spiritual resilience. He has grown stronger because of these two near-death medical conditions, as well as many other experiences through life. During his early school years, students and teachers marginalized and bullied him, calling him names like "Fatty Pflug" and "welfare trash."

In high school, he became a target for two teachers for reasons only known to them.

In his senior year of high school, he experienced further trauma when a dear friend he had faithfully protected from school bullies tragically lost his life in the 1985 Air India bombing.

After graduation, he went to the University of Guelph, where he played varsity football and wrestled. On the academic front, he pursued his education in hopes of one day being a police officer so he could "serve and protect."

In 1989 he secured that dream and joined the Guelph Police Service.

In 2006, he experienced a life-altering Post Traumatic Stress Injury (PTSI) after being unsuccessful in saving a two-year-old little girl who had drowned in the bathtub.

This event forced him to face his accumulated past personal and professional traumas and demons. Being aware that the self-realization and acceptance that he longed for could not be done alone, he sought out a PTSI counsellor named Mary Margaret. She collaborated diligently with him and helped him face his past. Through this incredibly caring and supportive environment, Doug could rediscover himself and be reacquainted with his service heart.

Doug now uses these experiences and life lessons learned along the way during his 35 years of accumulated time as a police officer, elite strength, and conditioning coach with Wrestle Canada, the Guelph Storm Hockey Club and Special Olympics Canada, and training/ mentoring athletes in the NHL, AHL, NCAA, OHL, National and ProvincialLevels to #RiseUpAndExcel.

Doug now coaches and mentors thousands, using the framework of his stress management and resiliency model, "Who Was I, Who Am I, and Who Do I Want to Be?" and "I Can, I Must, I Will."

This is an enlightening story of personal, physical, and emotional chaos. It demonstrates the building of resiliency, personal and professional growth, and triumph. It is a tale that Doug hopes will help others deal with their own experiences by using his tools to #RiseUpAndExcel

"FYG" BOOK REVIEWS

Review #1—Dr. Gary Marshall

Finding Your Granite: My Four Cornerstones of Personal Leadership is a moving and powerful memoir. The author, Doug Pflug, grew up in a small town in Southern Western Ontario, where from a very early age, he had to overcome unimaginable obstacles. Doug decided to attend university to escape the confines of small-town life, where his stint as a standout athlete led him to discover his real calling as a law enforcement officer. This memoir chronicles his internal struggle to understand his version of his life and to have the courage to step forward from his past. It offers a glimpse into a way of life that most of us will never experience, as well as an inspiring story about one man's capacity to rise up and excel. Read this book now!

Dr Gary Marshall
DBA—Leadership
www.linkedin.com/in/dr-gary-marshall-dba-1a57b2aa

Review #2—Adam Kinakin

Doug's story brought back many of the struggles I faced during my time with the Canadian Forces and post-service. It is a story that many veterans and public safety members share, and I am truly inspired by Doug and his ability to put that fight into words and his willingness and courage to share it with others. A key underlying principle to leadership displayed is that not all outstanding leaders are born but are created. Leadership is a journey that a select few navigate with the grace and humility that is showed in this book. A must-read for LEOs and public safety professionals.

Adam Kinakin
Founder, International Law Enforcement Training Network
https://podcast.ilet.network/show/tactical-breakdown/

Review #3—Chris D. Lewis

Reflecting on his life and career, Doug recounts the many events and people that shaped him. From a serious childhood illness, through school, his involvement in sports, coaching, and a successful police career—he learned from the good and from the bad along that journey. He presents his personal learnings and advice on resiliency and leadership from the heart, and additionally offers challenges to make the reader a better person and leader. A down-to-earth and enjoyable read!

Chris D. Lewis
OPP Commissioner (Ret.) and author of *Never Stop on a Hill*

Review #4—James Barker

Webster's dictionary symbolizes "granite" as possessing "unyielding firmness or endurance." Doug Pflug provides a blueprint for life based of real-life experiences from birth and how he utilized many of his life moments to create a legacy driven by the ideals of firmness and endurance. We all have life history and Doug tells his story like we are at a backyard barbecue—relaxed and sincere—in hopes we can identify with something that can help us as we create our own legacy.

James "Jim" Barker
Canadian Football League GM, VP and Coach: Four-time Grey Cup Champion. XFL Coach and Champion. TSN CFL Analyst.
https://en.wikipedia.org/wiki/Jim_Barker

Review #5—Rich Peverley

Doug and I met early in my career. He helped me set a base for hockey's physical demands. Never would I have guessed he was battling the demands of his job. Doug is an incredibly positive person, always presents himself with a smile and a joy to be around. When I asked him to assist me in presenting the Stanley Cup in Guelph, he jumped right onboard. Incredibly happy he has come out on top of his PTSI and helped others with the same battles.

Rich Peverley
7-year NHL veteran and Stanley Cup Champion with the Boston Bruins
https://g.co/kgs/cxbwE9

Review #6—Johnny Augustine

From life struggles, obstacles, adversity, and the darkness that Doug reveals. It is a testimony to who Doug is as a person and a mentor. Doug discusses and shares the events that he encountered as a young man that many people would not discuss. This says everything about him as a leader. A leader is not just someone who shows only their best and positive side, a leader is someone we can relate to. Doug is someone we can relate to because we all have our own personal battles that we do not share. We all need help and Doug discusses that countless times that we need to help each other and pick each other up. It's not a sign of weakness but a sign of strength. Amazing read and listen, thank you Doug for being an inspiration to many including myself.

Johnny Augustine
CFL veteran and Two Time Grey Cup Champion Winnipeg Blue Bombers
https://g.co/kgs/my1yxV

Review #7—Naomi Sneickus

Something happens when someone writes so openly and honestly about their life experiences, no matter how hard it is…The world breaks open, people lean forward and everyone who has ever had to deal with tough situations feel less alone. To me, Doug's display of that level of vulnerability is a display of amazing inner strength and a sign of a true leader. I knew Doug in high school as a cool football player who was a pretty big deal. Now I know him as a leader/author …and he's even a bigger deal!

Naomi Sneickus
Canadian Actress and Comedic Icon "Mr. D" on CBC
https://g.co/kgs/QCH1qx

Review #8—Sheila Good

Doug beckons us forward into our own self-discovery through the humble grace of his own story. Through humor and vulnerability, Doug ushers us into an opportunity for a perspective shift; encouraging us to embrace life's triumphs and tribulations as a crucible for transformation instead of destruction. His servant leadership motivates us to consider that our messes are perhaps a gate to explore a higher purpose. Doug inspires us to climb into the crucible of change instead of running for the hills and even if we have run for the hills… and felt that we've missed it… that it's never too late because every setback is just a setup for true success.

Sheila Good
International Speaker, Coach, Author and
Creator of Born to Influence.
Www.Bossladybizcoach.com

Notes:

Add your own notes in this space.

Index

Pages in *italics* refer to figures and pages in **bold** refer to tables

Printed in the United States
by Baker & Taylor Publisher Services